WHAT'S WRONG
with that MAN'S
HEAD

WHAT'S WRONG
with that MAN'S
HEAD

A l a n   J .   H e a t h

LitPrime Solutions
21250 Hawthorne Blvd
Suite 500, Torrance, CA 90503
www.litprime.com
Phone: 1 (209) 788-3500

Published by LitPrime Solutions   02/12/2021

ISBN: 978-1-953397-80-5(sc)
ISBN: 978-1-953397-81-2(hc)
ISBN: 978-1-953397-82-9(e)

Library of Congress Control Number: 2021900788

Contents

About the Author

Alan Heath grew up on a small dairy farm in the northwestern corner of Illinois. He received an undergraduate degree from Knox College and his Doctor of Dental Surgery from the University of Illinois. He is now retired and lives with his wife Cindy and their dog Coco in Frankfort, Illinois, where for forty years he ran a private practice dental office, entertaining his patients along the way.

About the Book

In a collection of essays drawn from daily life, Dr Alan Heath fills his first book with a hilarious account of life seen through the eyes of a dentist who never grew up. *What's Wrong with that Man's Head* takes us inside the mind of Dr Heath as he shares the stories of his first communion, taken at the insistence of his Mother-in-law (*Body of Christ*), of avoiding the bathroom while on his first date (*When Sphincters Relax*), and of an ill-advised ride in a rodeo (*A Mid-life Rodeo*). He struggles with the challenges of parenting, debating the legend of Santa Claus (*Yes, Virginia*), and losing a fifty-dollar bet to his five-year-old son (*Name That Tune*). And you'll laugh and cry at the same time as he shares the bittersweet tale of his mother-in-law's final moments (Last Words). His stories lead us on a fifty-year journey, and at the end, you may still wonder, "What's wrong with that man's head?"

Dedication

I would like to thank Cindy, the love of my life, and my stabilizing force. I fall in love with you again, every time I hear you laugh.

I met Cindy in college, and my first memory of her involves only her voice. I didn't find out until years later that *the voice* belonged to her.

It was our first day on campus, and I was fresh off the farm, away from home for the first time. Cow manure was literally still on my shoes.

About thirty students, all of us with the same faculty advisor, were gathered in a small lecture hall for an orientation meeting, and I wanted to be anywhere but there. The campus was calling to me. There was so much to do and see. There were tennis courts, and sidewalks, and buildings three stories tall. Things I had never seen before, and I wanted to get on with it.

Our faculty advisor finally finished his remarks, and if there were no questions, he said, we were free to go. I had pushed back my chair when a voice spoke up with a question. I don't recall the question, and I couldn't see who'd asked it, but the answer took another ten minutes out of my life. I was pushing back for a second time, when the voice piped up again. Another question. Another ten minutes. And, in case you're wondering, there was a third question.

The voice was Cindy's, of course, as I discovered years later while reminiscing with a group of college friends and causing Cindy to pipe up in an offended voice, "That was me!" and pointing out that she was simply asking all the questions that I and the others were too immature and irresponsible to ask ourselves.

From that day to this, she has been the responsible one, the grownup, in our relationship, and I admit freely that without Cindy, I would be living in a cardboard box under an overpass in the city. I'd like to think it would be a nice cardboard box, but still.

And thank you to my children, Corielle and Tony, who have brought so much joy into my life. We all hope for so many things for our children when they're born, but I've distilled my list down to a single wish. I wish for them to be happy. Whatever comes their way in life, may it make them as happy as they have made me in mine.

A special thank you to my daughter Corielle, the writer in the family, for her help in putting these stories into a readable form. If they still fall short of that, the fault is mine.

Thank you to Bill Moser, a friend and patient who lent his editing skills, and whose efforts, I hope, have kept Mrs. Hill, my old English teacher, from spinning in her grave.

Many friends and neighbors appear throughout these stories, and I would like to thank them all for enriching my life. I've been singularly blessed to have been surrounded by so many wonderful and remarkable people. I hope I've done them justice in these pages. I've changed the names in only a single story, and I'll leave it to you to guess which one. I apologize if you find yourself in here somewhere, and you don't remember things the same way I did, but these are my stories. If you remember things differently, write your own.

Prelude

I was going away to college in September. An important looking envelope had arrived in the mail and made it official. Inside was a letter of acceptance from Knox College, a small liberal arts school in Galesburg, Illinois. Small was an important modifier, because having grown up on a farm ten miles from Stockton, a town of less than two thousand people, I was afraid that anything approaching the size of the University of Illinois would swallow me whole. I might walk through the gates as a freshman and simply disappear, never to be seen or heard from again.

The year was 1972, and even in the small, scattered towns of rural northwestern Illinois, there were town kids and farm kids, and I was a farm kid. Today the distinction has blurred, but when I was young, life on a farm was different.

Our telephone, as one example, had a handle on the side that you cranked in order to reach the operator, who then placed your call. It was the sort of telephone that Sheriff Taylor used to call Aunt Bee in Mayberry. Incoming calls were announced in our house by two long rings followed by one short. Any other combination of rings was a call for one of the neighbors, but you were free to pick up and listen in, so long as you did it quietly.

And we didn't have an indoor bathroom until I was eight years old. We had water plumbed into the kitchen, but we didn't have anything that flushed or resembled a bathtub until 1962.

We took baths once a week, using water run into the kitchen sink. Our toilet was an outhouse a short walk up the hill. A longer and more perilous walk after dark. In the winter there was a chamber pot that sat at the top of the cellar steps, and it was carried to the outhouse once a day to be emptied.

If you're familiar with outhouses only from a picture you saw on a Christmas card that showed a picturesque little building mantled in snow behind a charming country house whose windows glowed a warm welcome to guests stepping out of a horse-drawn sleigh, allow me to burst your bubble. That little house was built of rough lumber, and there was a hornet's nest up under the eve. Inside was a bench seat that was nothing more than holes cut into a plank. There was never a single hole. Ours had two, but some had three or even four, and due to the danger of picking up a splinter, it was best not to slide off the seat when your business was finished. You did a straight lift.

There was no hanger on the wall dispensing a roll of scented two-ply tissue. There was a box filled with dry corn cobs. In the finer outhouses, there was a copy of the Sears and Roebuck catalogue that provided both reading material and a piece of paper. The outhouse was set over a hole dug into the ground, and when the hole was full, the little building was simply moved to a new location. I remember ours being moved only once, so it clearly took some time to fill the hole, even with six or eight people working at it full time.

The hole was deep and dark, and to my mind, ominous. I had concerns as to what might be lurking down there. Spiders certainly. Snakes possibly, and the thought of my bare and undefended hindquarters exposed to those dangers added spice to my visits. I know I wasn't the only one who entertained such thoughts, because on one occasion I crept up behind the outhouse while it was occupied by my father, and I passed a long stick through a knothole low on the back wall of the outhouse. With a quick upward poke, I caused my dad to erupt through the front door of the outhouse with his pants still around his ankles. I don't think anyone could have moved so far or so fast if the thought of spiders and snakes hadn't already been in their minds.

Our family was medium sized, by farm standards. There were eight of us all together. I had older twin sisters, a twin brother, and two much younger sisters, all of us crowded into an old farmhouse with two small bedrooms. There was a room on the first floor that was originally a parlor, and that was where my parents slept. The two bedrooms were upstairs, and those were for my twin sisters and my brother and me. When my younger sisters came along, dad built a small addition that served as a combination bedroom and storage room, and they bunked in there.

It was a wonderful life in a house of noisy togetherness. Living so far from any neighbors, much less the nearest town, we were our own friends and companions. We made up our own games. We played "Butterfly tag" where we ran around the yard trailing blankets that flew behind us like giant wings. We pushed enormous tractor tires to the top of the hill and rolled down inside the tires. We built forts and tunnels from haybales up in the haymow. We made lanterns from fireflies captured in mason jars. And we worked, from an early age. In the fields, in the barn, and in the garden. By the time we were eight we were driving tractors in the fields. We were up before six in the morning to bring the cows in to milk, and, after working a full day, we milked them again before coming in for supper at eight.

And now, as I held the letter from Knox College in my hand, I knew I was leaving this behind. I had decided that farming was not for me. My twin brother was staying behind and might end up going into partnership with dad, but I was moving on. I had no plan beyond moving on, and I didn't know what the future held, what lay in store for me. But I knew it would be different.

What's Wrong with that Man's Head?

The little girl in front of me in the check-out line at the local grocery store stared at me with frank fascination. Maybe, I thought with a little swell of pride, she even recognized me. It was a small town, after all, and I was the new dentist. I gave her a smile and a little wave. Finally, she tugged on her mother's skirt and whispered in that voice a child uses that can be heard all the way back in Produce, "Mommy, what's wrong with that man's head?"

Well, maybe she didn't recognize me after all, but I was still the new dentist, and that had to count for something.

I wasn't born wanting to be a dentist, if you've ever wondered about how that sort of thing comes about. Oh sure, I pulled the wings off a couple of flies, but that didn't mean anything. I was young. And they were flies.

No, I wanted to be a farmer when I grew up, like my father, and his father, and I might have done it too, if farming hadn't involved so much actual labor. That was the deal breaker, really. The labor. Especially in the winter, when the cows stayed in the barn, and you had to grind corn out of a frozen crib to feed them, and everything you fed them came out the other end magically multiplied and transformed and had to be shoveled away again. It was all just too much.

I went away to college, and then to dental school, and eventually I found my way to Frankfort, where I sat now behind an empty reception desk in my soon-to-be dental office, waiting for the delivery of my shiny new dental equipment.

I was twenty-seven years old, but I had the fresh face of an eighth grader, and I was regularly carded not only for alcohol but for the bingo cards they gave out at grocery stores. While I was in Dental school, I grew a mustache in order to look older and more professional. But it was a sorry affair and fooled no one, so I shaved it off.

My office was in a building on the main road that passed through Frankfort Illinois, a sleepy little village south of Chicago that was in the process of deciding if it wanted to remain a farm town or evolve into a bedroom community for young professionals who worked in the city. My office space was outfitted with the usual amenities, desks, cabinets, carpet. All I needed to begin my new career was a dental chair and an x-ray machine, and the delivery man was due any minute.

I glanced up from my book as a man came in the front door. I looked at him expectantly, and he nodded briefly in my direction but said nothing. He looked from the reception area into the main office, looked at me again, shrugged his shoulders, and walked out.

Thirty minutes later, he came back in, this time looking annoyed. Again he nodded to me, silently looked around the empty office, and stomped back out, mumbling to himself. Another fifteen minutes passed, and he was back again, clearly irate. He leaned through the open window that led from the reception area to where I sat, and craned his neck in all directions. Finally he settled a belligerent glare on me.

"Do you have any idea," he asked with exasperation, "when the dentist is going to get here?"

That turned out to be a common refrain among my early patients. They entered my office on the occasion of their initial appointment, followed my assistant to the dental chair, saw me for the first time, and looked around wildly, as if hoping to find a hidden camera. I honestly don't know why any of them stayed, but to test the mettle of those that did, I had braces put onto my teeth during my first year in practice.

It was as if, in an effort to look even younger, I'd dressed up as a teenager, and the braces were the elaborate touch that completed the disguise. And, in case anyone may have missed the point, I also wore a headgear.

Thankfully, you don't see headgear much anymore, but mine was fastened by a series of elastic straps to a beanie that sat on the top and back of my head. It pulled on my teeth by means of a large metal bow that jutted out of my mouth like the antennae on an old TV set. As if by putting your ear close enough to my head, you might actually hear that I was listening to an episode of *I Love Lucy*.

Inside the dental office my appliance, although grotesque, was tolerable. Headgear on the dentist might be considered a curiosity, or maybe a conversation starter, but in line at the grocery store?

The little girl stared with open-mouthed amazement until she finally tugged at her mother's skirt. "Mommy," she whispered, "what's wrong with that man's head?"

Mommy, of course, had been politely averting her eyes from my disfigurement, but now, confronted by her child's question, she glanced at me apologetically. "Don't stare Honey," she whispered back. "He's been in an accident."

"That's what I love about children," people say, "they're so honest." Well, I personally don't care for honesty. Several years later, another six-year-old girl was standing in my waiting room before her appointment. Knowing she was nervous and hoping to put her at ease, I stuck my head through the doorway as I passed. "Hi, Sweetheart," I called out in my friendliest voice, "You're next!" She looked up with startled eyes and promptly threw up onto my carpet.

I know she was being honest, but still, I could have done without it. After you see enough of that sort of thing, you start to wonder if maybe everyone doesn't feel the same, and most are just too polite to throw up.

Little Sonnet Corkery, four years old, was in for her very first visit and sat through her entire appointment without making a sound. Her silence was not a comfortable silence. Hers was a hostile, accusatory silence. The kind of silence that resisted all my efforts at conversation. The kind of silence that filled a room. By the end of her appointment, as I led her from the chair to the front desk, her silence was all I could hear.

At the front desk, I played my final card, which had never failed to win over even the most reluctant children. I presented her with our large plastic Prize Bucket filled with inexpensive toys. If the author of *How to Make Friends and Influence People* didn't mention a large plastic bucket of toys, he should have. By the time kids finished pawing through the bucket, I was their best friend.

Sonnet, though, was a tougher nut. She hid behind her mother's skirt with her face pressed into folds of fabric and refused to even look at the bucket. Still no sound passed her lips. I finally gave up and was turning to my next patient when she peeked from behind her mother's dress and spoke for the first and only time.

"You big jerk!" she said with a childish lisp.

I was finally forced to accept a fact that should have been obvious from the start. People don't like the dentist, and even the grownups won't hesitate to tell you.

The big, burly biker sitting in my chair with sweat on his upper lip and alcohol on his breath looked me right in the eye. "You know, Doc," he said, "no offense, but I hate dentists."

"That's all right," I said. "I don't care for bikers, myself."

No! Of course I didn't say that. I would never say that. It would be rude, and besides, did I mention he was big and burly and half drunk? No, I went on about my business, shot him full of Novocain, and kept my personal likes and dislikes to myself.

When his appointment was over, the biker stood at the front desk with a string of drool hanging from his lip. He had a spot of blood on his chin and a bad taste in his mouth that he couldn't quite identify, and he said, "Thank you, Doc."

Thank you? If you work in any other profession, and at the end of the day you have a client in that condition, somebody's going to jail. This guy could have had me up on charges for the mysterious bad taste alone, and yet he said thank you.

It was that moment, and others like it, that made me glad I'd left the farm. On the farm, even after all the grinding and feeding and milking and shoveling, there's never a thank you. A cow is an ungrateful beast.

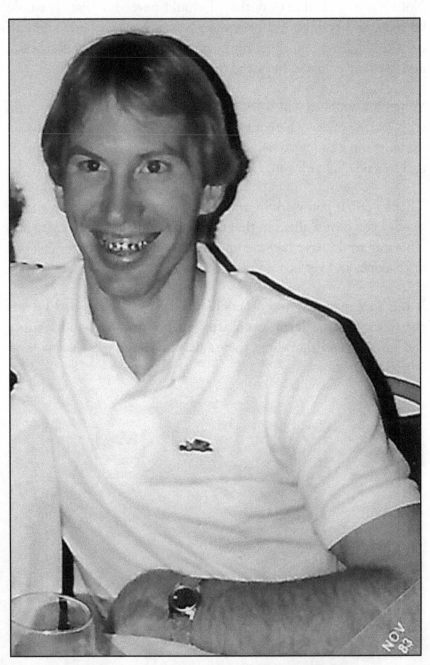

This is me with my braces. You'll forgive me, but I never allowed a picture to be taken with the headgear.

I Used to Wrestle

I used to wrestle, back in the day. I don't anymore, but I used to, and in fact, that's how Cindy and I met. It's a common enough story, and one you've heard a thousand times. Boy meets girl. Boy wrestles girl.

But I'm getting ahead of myself. Let me start over.

I started wrestling as a high school freshman, and I continued all through college. In fact, when it came time to choose among colleges, I was offered some wrestling scholarships. Luckily, I didn't accept any of those offers, or I never would have met Cindy, and my story would have had a completely different ending.

I weighed only seventy-five pounds when I first put on a wrestling uniform back in 1968. I was recruited by my friends to join the team at midseason, because their light-weight wrestler had been injured, and they needed someone small to take his place. I was the smallest person anyone knew.

It's hard for people to visualize just how small a boy of seventy-five pounds is. By way of comparison, you've lost more weight while sitting on a toilet. The lightest weight class was ninety-five pounds, and I was twenty pounds underweight. During the weigh-in before matches, I didn't bother to take off my clothes. While everyone else stepped out of their underwear to see if they'd lost that last fraction of a pound, I jumped onto the scales with my winter coat on. Our uniform's smallest size was too large for me by far. There was a very real danger that my opponent and I, like kittens playing with a ball of yarn, might become tangled in the excess material. To avoid that embarrassment, Coach gathered all the loose fabric into a wad between my shoulders and wrapped it with duct tape. I looked like a wind-up toy.

Simply saying that I lost all my matches during that first year doesn't do the matter justice. My bouts were more along the lines of being picked on by a school-yard bully. I didn't just lose. My opponents took my lunch money, followed me into the locker room, and stuck my head into a toilet. It's a wonder the Principal didn't run onto the mat and intervene on my behalf.

When I went away to college, I still tipped the scales at just under one hundred and twenty pounds, and that's when I met Cindy.

During the first days of our freshman year, Cindy and a small group of girls dropped by the Conger residence hall in the Men's Quad, where my suitemates and I were getting acquainted with one another. Boys of that age becoming acquainted involve rituals that are complex and steeped in tradition. There's a lot of posturing and strutting. If you can imagine *Lord of the Flies* without the pig, it's like that. Boys establish rank within a social group by showing off. If you have a skill, you trot it out, and the more impressive your skill, the more status you gain. Ken Butterworth juggled ping-pong balls, and Steve Miller showed us how to pass gas and set it on fire. Both demonstrations were impressive, but Steve gained higher status.

The most common way of showing off, though, is through physical combat, and when someone inevitably began to push the furniture aside to make room for a wrestling competition, my heart leapt. Cindy's dark-eyed beauty had already caught my eye, and maybe I couldn't juggle or light farts, but I could wrestle! Not only was I going to gain status within the group, I was going to show off in front of Cindy.

But there's no glory to be gained by wrestling the smallest guy, and I was easily the smallest guy in the room. While the others paired off to wrestle, I was left leaning against the wall in frustration. Watching. Finally, it was decided that I should be given the opportunity to wrestle one of the girls. The thinking was that I was little, and the girls were little, and it would be amusing. Like watching midgets wrestle.

Cindy was chosen as my opponent. She certainly didn't volunteer. She was simply the one who came the nearest to being as small as I was, and so we squared off in the center of the room. Now, if you're thinking that I took advantage of this situation, vis-à-vis rolling around on the floor with a nubile young woman, well, shame on you! The thought never occurred to me. To my way of thinking, my showing off would remain the same, but Cindy now had a seat on the court, so to speak.

I took her down with a near-ankle sweep. I grabbed her ankle and pulled it sideways while quickly lifting it above her head. Her second foot left the ground, and we both fell to the floor. The near-ankle sweep is a simple take-down, elegant and dramatic, and I chose it because I hoped it would make a good first impression on Cindy. Unfortunately, a ripping noise accompanied us to the floor. A smarter man would have paused to assess the extent of the damage, but I flowed immediately into my next move, a cross-body leg ride, and from there into a Guillotine pinning combination. In far less time than it's taken to tell, Cindy was twisted into a position she would have declared impossible only a moment before, and the match was over.

The Guillotine ends with one of your opponent's legs locked, and their body twisted as if it were a chicken bone and someone was about to make a wish. The finish was made even more dramatic since Cindy's jeans had ripped down the inseam only seconds before.

Our match was a resounding success, from my perspective, but Cindy wasn't as impressed as I'd hoped. For the longest time she acted as if she didn't like me at all, and more than a year passed before we began to date. Eventually though, she came to admire the way I looked in my singlet, and we were engaged to be married by the time of our graduation four years later.

Wrestling isn't a sport one can continue after leaving the collegiate programs. You can play football in your backyard on Thanksgiving Day. Or you can find a volleyball game on the beach behind any resort hotel, and nobody minds. But if you wrestle, and you go to the high school and ask if you can roll around with the boys? All of a sudden, I need a restraining order?

So, like I said, I used to wrestle, back in the day, but I don't anymore.

Body of Christ

I was raised a Methodist, in a little one room country church that stood on the banks of a creek that meandered through the valley below our farm. My family sat in the third pew from the back on the right-hand side of the aisle. There were numerous empty pews in front of ours, but Methodists prefer to huddle in the rear of the sanctuary, as if there's about to be a fire and not everyone will get out. In the Methodist Church, when we sing a hymn, we sing all the verses. We say all the words to the Lord's Prayer, even the last part, and we take communion on Communion Sunday.

Communion Sunday is a special day, held twice a year, and it involves getting a warm hunk of bread, torn from a freshly baked loaf, and a personal serving of grape juice poured into a small, silver cup and presented on a silver tray.

Then I married Cindy, who, as it turned out, was not a Methodist. She was a Catholic, and although marrying a Catholic did not require that I convert, it did require that I pledge to raise my children in the mysteries of the Catholic faith, which is how I came to find myself attending Mass on Sunday mornings.

One of the mysteries of the Catholic faith, I came to discover, is that every Sunday is Communion Sunday. Week after week, I watched as a line formed and processed down the aisle to receive a thin wafer, stamped out by the millions in a bakery in the basement of the Vatican, and a sip of wine from a shared cup. Communion in the Catholic church, I learned, was one of the Seven Holy Sacraments, and it was made clear to me that I was not welcomed to participate in this ritual, because I wasn't confirmed into the Catholic faith. But even without that restriction I would have been hesitant to join in, because, as I pointed out before, they all drank from the same cup. Granted, it was a nice cup. It was more of a goblet really, and it was probably too costly for everyone to have their own, but in spite of the fact that the priest rotated the cup one quarter turn after each supplicant and wiped the edge with a little cloth, by my calculation every fourth person had put their lips onto the same spot, and who knew where that person had been? Everyone today knows that if you take communion with one person, you're taking communion with every person that person has ever taken communion with.

So, I would happily have lived my entire life without taking communion in the Catholic church, but Cindy's mother was of a different mind. She somehow felt a personal responsibility for the salvation of my immortal soul, and she felt that the best place to begin was at the Cup of Communion.

"Come on Alan," she coaxed whenever we joined her at Mass, "take communion with me this Sunday."

"No, Mom," I demurred. "You know they don't want me to take a sacrament when I haven't been confirmed. Lightning might strike me dead."

Apparently, that was a risk she was willing to take, and Sunday after Sunday, as months grew into years, she kept after me. Finally, a time came when we were all on vacation together in Florida, and we found ourselves in an unfamiliar church in Sarasota.

"Alan," Mom whispered, "Come up to communion with me today."

"Mom –" She cut me off.

"No one knows you here," she continued. "No one will know you're not Catholic."

"God will know," I pointed out.

"God doesn't care," she explained. "Only the Catholic church cares, and we won't tell them."

Well, that argument made a lot of sense to me. I could almost imagine Martin Luther's mother-in-law whispering it to him, so I finally let myself be convinced and slid out of my seat to join Cindy and her Mom in the long line heading to the front of the church.

As we slowly advanced, I prepared myself for the administration of my first Holy Sacrament by mimicking the posture of those around me. I bowed my head and held my hands folded and slightly raised in an attitude of reverent reflection.

I watched carefully as those at the front of the line received the Host, and I noted that there were two methods. The first was to hold out the cupped hands to receive the wafer, then transfer it into the mouth and follow with a quick Sign of the Cross, which seemed to be up, down, left, and then right. I had reservations regarding this method because there was the possibility of mishandling the Host.

The second method was simpler, and, at the same time, more traditional. When the supplicant came to the front of the line, the priest held the wafer up for their inspection. They then opened their mouths, and he laid the Host directly onto their tongue. They went immediately into the Sign of the Cross - up, down, left, right - and moved on to the cup, which appeared to be optional and which, in the interest of hygiene, I intended to skip.

As I approached the head of the line, I went over the Sign of the Cross, rehearsing the movements with tiny motions of a single finger of my folded hands. Up, down, left, right. I watched Cindy and her mother take their turns in front of the priest, and then stepped up myself. "Up, down, left, right," I repeated soundlessly in my head as the priest held the wafer in front of my eyes. I gave it a critical look and opened my mouth. To my astonishment, rather than placing the Host onto my tongue, the priest pulled back his hand and looked at me quizzically.

I had done something wrong! But what could it be?

I watched as the priest once again held the wafer before my eyes.

Perhaps I hadn't inspected the Host carefully enough, or opened wide enough, so I leaned forward slightly, gave the Host a thorough looking over, and opened my mouth more fully, pushing my tongue out a bit. Again, the priest withdrew his hand and looked at me with reproach. He suspected! Somehow he knew that I was a Methodist and unworthy of the Holy Sacraments of the Catholic Church! And yet, once again he held the Host in front of my eyes, now almost as if he were taunting me with it.

This time I heard him say, as he presented the wafer, "Body of Christ."

Well, yes, I thought. I knew that was the general idea. This time I leaned forward at the waist and put my tongue out fully, as if I intended to lick the wafer from his fingers, and he stepped back in alarm, keeping the wafer just out of my reach. He looked at me now with his suspicions confirmed.

"Body of Christ," he repeated more firmly. It occurred to me now for the first time that he might be waiting for a response of some sort; a secret Catholic countersign perhaps, but what could it be?

"Please?" I ventured hopefully, although, with my mouth gaped open and my tongue fully protruded, I suspect I was hard to understand.

The priest sighed sadly and finally laid the wafer onto my outstretched tongue. My mouth was so dry at this point that when I returned to my pew the Host still lay in my mouth like a disk of notebook paper.

Cindy and her mother, who had long since returned to their seats and had been watching with fascination and mounting concern as the drama unfolded at the front of the Church, turned to me at once. "What happened?" they whispered. "What took you so long?"

"He knew!" I said through a spray of Host.

"He knew what?"

"He knew I was a Methodist," I explained, "and he wouldn't give me the Host! He kept pulling it away. He made me beg!"

"He made you beg?" they asked in unified disbelief.

"He kept telling me it was the Body of Christ," I said, "and he wouldn't give it to me until I said please."

They both dissolved into that silent, quaking laugh that people do when they're in church or at a funeral. "No," Cindy finally explained, "He says 'Body of Christ' and you say 'Amen', and *then* he gives it to you!"

Well, someone could have told me that sooner, I thought.

"And then," Cindy's mom added, "you're supposed to make the Sign of the Cross. You didn't make the Sign of the Cross."

Damn! It's a wonder lightning didn't strike me dead.

Please Don't Judge Me

A familiar looking young woman came running up as I walked off the field at the end of the football game. I had just joined a team in the Park District's Touch Football league, and I hadn't yet met all of the guys or their significant others.

"Dr. Heath?" she called. "Dr Heath? It is you, isn't it? Oh my god! I'm so happy to see you! Did you move to Frankfort? Are you going to be starting a practice here?"

Suddenly I recognized her, and I knew this wasn't going to end well.

******

Cindy and I had just moved to Frankfort from an apartment which stood just across the parking lot from Michael Reese Hospital, where I had spent the past year in a General Practice Dental Residency program. A dental residency is an optional and prestigious year after graduation from Dental school, and there are only a few programs like the one at Michael Reese. Spots are few and hard to qualify for, and those selected are rewarded with a grueling year of long days and sleepless nights.

We worked in the hospital Dental Clinic during the day and answered calls in the Emergency Room at night. In the clinic we gained additional experience, competence, and confidence in a vast array of dental procedures, and in the Emergency Room we learned skills that we might never use, but we became better dentists for having made the effort.

We did intubation and airway management in trauma and cardiac cases, and when someone came in with facial lacerations, from a slip and fall, a car accident, or a knife fight, we did the suturing. There were Plastic Surgeons on staff, but they didn't answer Emergency Room call, so unless a nose had to be sewn back on, we did the suture work.

Michael Reese was a fine hospital, with a reputation for excellent patient care, but it was not the sort of place you went unless you were prepared to have every effort made on your behalf. It was a teaching hospital, and so they taught... on you. On one of my nights in the ER, a woman came in Code Blue - cardiac arrest. She had suffered a heart attack in a high-rise apartment building, and there had been a long delay in the response of the ambulance and paramedics, so that by the time she arrived in the emergency room, she had been dead for almost an hour. Not to be swayed from our duties by a minor technicality, we began CPR as she was being intubated, and then her chest was opened, and the medical team did open chest cardiac massage before she was finally pronounced dead.

It might sound callous, I know, or even macabre, but it was a teaching hospital, and while the residents were going through the motions of trying to revive a woman who was clearly already gone, they were also gaining proficiencies that would help them save the next person who came through their doors.

In addition to the Dental Clinic and Emergency Room call, Dental Residents did a two-month rotation in General Anesthesia. For the first week we had the assistance of a Nurse Anesthetist and the watchful eye of an Attending Anesthesiologist, but after that, we were on our own. The medicine was straight-forward, and once we were comfortable with the processes, it was challenging and fun.

We visited the patients scheduled for surgery the night before to do medical evaluations and answer any of their pre-opp questions. We listened to their hearts and lungs, reviewed their medical histories, and then saw them the next day in the operating room. There we started their IV lines, hooked up their monitors, pushed the drugs that put them to sleep, then intubated, and managed their breathing during the procedure. At the end of it all, we pushed more drugs to reverse the effects of the first, and accompanied them to the recovery room, where we finally left them in the hands of the nursing staff.

At first, it was uncomfortable, doing anesthesia, 'real medicine', when all our training had been of the dental variety, but, after a few patients it became routine, and it didn't occur to any of us to wonder what the patients might have thought if they'd known we were recently graduated dental students rather than medical residents. We certainly didn't point the fact out, and unless you looked very closely at the ID badges we wore, which were labeled DDS rather than MD, no one was the wiser.

One night during my rotation, I was doing pre-opp rounds. I was long past the point of being uncomfortable in my white lab coat and blue scrubs, and I walked around with a stethoscope draped around my neck, looking and acting for all the world like a Real Doctor. I walked into the room with a chart held under my arm.

"Hello," I said. "I'm Doctor Heath. I'm going to be doing the anesthesia for your procedure tomorrow."

I was addressing a nervous young woman who was scheduled to have a breast lump removed the next day. I talked for a moment to put her at ease before I opened her chart and reviewed her medical history and current medications. Then I took her blood pressure, listened to her heart and lungs, and all the while she continued to chatter nervously.

She was from the southern suburbs, I learned, where she kept a horse at a stable, and in fact, that was how she had become aware of her breast lump. While she was riding her horse, she said, the motion of the ride caused her breasts to move in a way that had made her aware of an odd feeling, and self-exam had allowed her to find a small mass.

By the time I was finished with my exam, she was winding up her story, and she had calmed considerably. "I'm so happy I got to talk with you, Dr. Heath," she said. "I was so nervous. I just wish I knew what this lump was. It's just here," she continued, and she put a finger onto her chest. "Would you like to feel it?"

Now, please don't judge me. I know I was just a dentist, and you know I was just a dentist, but we were in a teaching hospital, and I had watched cardiac massage being performed on a dead woman. This was just another teaching moment.

I palpated carefully and felt the small, movable lump that she was going to have removed the next day. After a moment I stepped back. "You know what?" I said, "I don't think you have anything to worry about. To me that feels like a benign fibrous mass, and I would expect that you're going to be completely fine after tomorrow."

"Oh, thank you so much Dr. Heath!" she effused. "I hope you're right. You've made me feel so much better."

I saw her the next day in surgery, and her procedure went smoothly. The surgeon removed a small fibrous mass, and she was sent home the following day.

I didn't see her again until she ran up to me on the football field six months later.

"Dr Heath?" she called. "Dr Heath? It is you, isn't it! Oh my god! I'm so happy to see you. Have you moved to Frankfort? Are you going to set up a practice in the area? If you are, I want to be your first patient!"

She was truly delighted to see me. So much so, in fact, that I was concerned she might insist I feel her breast again, and I stepped back quickly.

"It's great to see you," I said. "You're doing well?"

"Yes, I'm fine. It was nothing, just like you said. Are you going to start a practice nearby?"

"Yes, I am," I admitted. "I've just opened a Dental office in Frankfort."

Her face fell, and there was a long pause as wheels turned in her head.

"You're a dentist?" she asked.

"Yes I am."

"Oh," she said, and she turned and walked away.

But it was a teaching hospital, and if I ever need to know what a fibrous mass feels like, now I know.

You're judging me, aren't you.

Primordial Urges

Cindy and I bought our first home when we moved to Frankfort in 1981. It was a two-story townhouse in an area just outside of town that was known for being nice, but affordable. The realtor described our new home as cozy but having just moved from a small one-bedroom apartment in the city, to us it was luxurious. In fact, we felt like Landed Gentry, and if the townhouse had been about three hundred square feet larger, I would have insisted that people start referring to me as Squire Heath.

Shortly after we moved in, we had friends over for dinner, and while Cindy took the women on a tour of the upstairs to admire the way she'd buried our bed with pillows, I took the men into the basement.

In case you've ever wondered, basements are where we men go while you ladies tour the upstairs. We like it down there. It's like a cave, and it harkens back to our primordial roots, like the mournful sound of wolves howling at night. There are caves in France with ancient drawings of elk on the walls, and in modern homes there are basements with framed pictures of dogs playing poker. It's the same thing. No woman ever hung a picture of a dog playing poker, and it wasn't a woman who painted the prehistoric elk. If you look closely, the elk has a spear sticking out of its side. A man painted that picture, and then he sat down in front of it and did whatever it was men did before there was football to watch on TV.

Men will gather in the basement and admire the furnace, if that's all that's down there, but we prefer over-stuffed chairs in front of a big screen TV. Throw in a dart board and carpet that absorbs spilled chili without anyone being the wiser, and we'll ask for nothing more.

Our townhouse had a tiny basement. It was dark and unfinished, but for weeks I sat at the foot of the stairs, lost in admiration, yet intrigued by how much more it might become. I had never attempted a home remodeling project, and the prospect was daunting. Still, the Primordial Urges of Man - food, sex, and basement remodeling - are irresistible, so I eventually took my courage in one hand and my tape measure in the other and began making sketches on a pad of paper. When my plans were complete, I carried them to Fox Lumber.

I strode purposefully to the counter where Orville Bell stood, dressed in his uniform of loose-fitting bib overalls and a plaid flannel shirt. Orville was a fixture at the local lumber store, and if he owned a second flannel shirt or another pair of overalls, I never saw them. "I'm going to finish my basement," I announced proudly, "and I'll need two-by-fours and some paneling."

"All right," Orville said, licking the tip of his pencil and touching it to a pad of paper, "how many two-by-fours do you need?"

Well, I hadn't really thought as far as actual numbers.

"It's a smallish basement," I volunteered.

"Ok. Are you putting your studs on sixteen-inch centers? Then we could figure how many linear feet of wall you've got and go from there."

"Yeah," I ventured, not wanting to appear totally clueless. "Sure. Sixteen-inch centers. If you think that's best. Hey," I added, as if struck by a sudden thought, "I've got a drawing here of what I thought I'd do."

"All right," Orville said, fixing me with a suspicious stare. "Are you going to want construction grade?"

I was starting to hyperventilate. If there were grades, I supposed I wanted a good one, but there was no point in being wasteful. "It's just for the basement," I reminded him. "What are my choices?"

"Listen Doc," he said, finally taking pity on me. "Let me see that paper you got there." He inspected my notes carefully, all the while talking under his breath in a low monotone. Occasionally he looked up and asked me a question.

"How are you planning to fasten the sill plates to the floor?"

I shrugged.

"Are you going to bend pipe or use Romex?"

I answered with a blank stare.

He soon stopped asking and simply filled my sheet of paper with notes and scribbles. By the time I left for home, Orville had taken well over one thousand of my dollars and set me up with everything I needed.

It was a job that would have taken a qualified carpenter two days, but I worked on the project for six months. I often disappeared into the basement and spent hours sitting at the foot of the stairs, trying to figure out how to manage a particularly pesky problem. After reaching a decision, I would return upstairs, feeling triumphant, only to be met by Cindy.

"I didn't hear any hammering down there."

"Well," I would answer, "I didn't actually *do* anything, per se, but I did figure out how to box in the sewer pipe that runs along the wall by the stairs."

"You were down there for two hours!"

"I was thinking."

I eventually finished, of course, and when I did, I took great pride in giving tours of my basement to anyone who came to visit. From the three-way switch in the stairwell, to the alcove, custom built to fit my sofa, I was a proud father showing off his first-born. But I found that I wasn't able show my creation without pointing out its flaws. I was literally incapable of leading you through my basement without highlighting how I'd screwed it up. Even if it was something you would never have noticed on your own, I called it to your attention with brutal honesty.

"See over there?" I would admit dolefully. "I got off level with the outer track for the suspended ceiling. Stand just here and you can see it."

I discovered later that this was a trait shared by men everywhere, and I wondered at this universal tendency. Then it occurred to me that the flaws we point out are where we ran into difficulties, and we overcame them. We're not apologizing, we're bragging.

If you ever get to France, go stand in that ancient cave and listen carefully. Whispering down through the corridors of time, you may hear the echo of two men's voices.

"Come look at this drawing I made of an Elk."

"Oooh! That's a nice Elk."

"Yes, but see how it has only three legs?"

"Oh, I hadn't noticed, but now you say it, it does look like it's falling down."

"That's why I added the spear."

"Ahh! That was smart."

"Thanks... Hey, do you want to sit on these big rocks and watch the bears?"

Turkey at the Last Supper

It was the morning of Thanksgiving Day, and Cindy and I were dressing for dinner when the phone rang. It was my brother Dale, who was driving a semi-truck loaded with frozen meat from Omaha to New York. He was close to Frankfort, he said, and he wondered if we had room for one more at our table so he wouldn't have to eat turkey loaf at a truck stop in Indiana.

"Absolutely!" I said without hesitation. "We're eating at Peppy's house. There's always room for one more."

In the early years of our marriage, Cindy's brother Joe, who everyone called Peppy, invited us to his house each year for Thanksgiving dinner. The group generally included Peppy and his wife Andy, their four children, Cindy's mom and dad, her Aunt Ang, Andy's mom, her Aunt Dorothy, and often Peppy's friend Steve, who, for reasons unknown, was often in attendance at holiday dinners.

I hung up the phone and turned to Cindy. "Guess what!" I said. "Dale's coming for dinner. He'll be here in about a half hour."

Cindy gave me a skeptical look. "Did you remember that we're eating at Peppy's Country Club this year," she asked, "instead of at his house?"

Well, of course I hadn't remembered that. It takes all my mental powers to remember to put the toilet seat down and wash my hands. There's no room left in my head for a change of Thanksgiving's dinner plans.

We soon had Peppy on the phone. "Of course he's welcome," Peppy said. "Just make sure he wears a jacket. That's club policy."

I pointed out that I was certain Dale didn't carry a sport coat in the cab of the truck. In fact, I was fairly confident that he didn't own one, or a pair of dress shoes for that matter. Dale was a meat and potatoes guy.

"Well, he can't show up wearing Carhartts," Peppy said. "You guys are twins, right? Give him a jacket of yours to wear."

Two hours later, as we walked through the main entrance to Olympia Fields, Dale was squeezed into a powder blue sport coat that I had worn to a Pi Phi Formal when Cindy and I were in college. The seams of the jacket were holding themselves together across his shoulders, but if you looked closely you could count the individual threads.

Dale had objected when he learned of the jacket requirement, but when we told him that it was the price of a turkey dinner, and that he could hang it on the back of his chair as soon as he got inside, he agreed to the inconvenience. Now, so long as he didn't take a full breath or reach for anything in front of him, he cut a dashing figure.

We were milling around the table sipping drinks when Peppy told us that Cindy's dad would be coming alone this year. "Mom's caught a head cold," he said with a shrug. "Or maybe the flu. She says she doesn't want to go out while she's contagious."

Cindy's family was Italian, or Sicilian, to be more precise, and anyone who has ever watched *Everybody Loves Raymond* knows Cindy's mom. Not only did she look so exactly like Ray's mother Marie that she was frequently stopped for autographs, but she had every one of Marie's tics and quirks. She was a prideful cook. Her gnocchi and lasagna were legendary. She covered her sofa with clear plastic, and whenever she came to our house, she scrubbed that hard-to-reach spot on the bathroom floor behind the toilet bowl and then whispered to Cindy, "I cleaned your bathroom floor. It was dirty." She disapproved of peanut butter and jelly, which was what lazy mothers served their kids for lunch, and she loved her children completely and martyred herself for them regularly.

That she was now coming down with the flu, in fact, may or may not have been true, and Peppy had his doubts. Mom had clear notions concerning a daughter-in-law's responsibilities when hosting the family for Thanksgiving dinner and having lunch at the Club did not measure up. Since Andy had also fallen short more than once on the peanut butter and jelly issue, it was just possible that Mom's illness was more of a sulk.

As we all began to find seats around the table, Andy noticed her mother and Aunt Dorothy with their heads together counting chairs, and after a brief word with them, she leaned over to Peppy. "We're going to have to ask our waitress to divide us into two tables," she said. "With Dale, and counting Dad when he gets here, there will be thirteen at this table, and Aunt Dorothy won't sit at a table of thirteen. It's bad luck."

"Are you kidding me?" Peppy asked. "The room is packed. They don't have room to split a table."

"Well," Andy explained, "we have to do something. It goes back to the Last Supper. If there are thirteen at a table, one of those people won't be alive the next year."

The waitress, in response to a quiet inquiry, confirmed Peppy's fear that she could not split the table, and she politely declined an invitation to make it a table of fourteen by joining the family for dinner. Peppy knew that the solution to his dilemma was at home with the flu, and he grabbed a phone. Dad answered, and, after Peppy explained about the table of thirteen, he went to talk to Mom.

No, he said, coming back to the phone, Mom still wasn't feeling well enough to come to the club. "Ok, I'll come talk to her myself," Peppy said. "In the meantime, try once more yourself. Tell her she has to come." The house was only a short distance away, and Peppy was there in less than ten minutes. He was met at the door by Dad, who had his coat draped over his arm. Mom still wasn't coming.

A voice drifted down from the head of the stairs leading to the bedrooms. "Hi Peppy," Mom quavered in the pitiful voice of someone calling in sick to work. "How is everything at the Club, Honey?" Peppy went to the foot of the stairs and looked up. Mom stood there wearing a purple robe over a floral night dress. A pink scarf was wrapped twice around her throat, and fuzzy slippers covered her white cotton socks. She wore no makeup and smelt of Vicks VapoRub. Her hair had been slept in.

"Mom," Peppy said, seizing the initiative, "didn't Dad tell you we need you to come to the Country Club for dinner? Why aren't you getting ready?"

Mom turned white with indignation. "Why aren't I getting ready? *Why aren't I getting ready?* You want I should get up from my sick bed and go to your fancy Country Club and eat with strangers? A woman as sick as I am should go out because your wife has superstitious relatives?" She shook her fist and looked at the ceiling. "How selfish is my son that he would ask his mother to do this?" And she turned and retreated into her bedroom.

Peppy took the steps two at a time and carried the battle onto the second floor. "You're not really sick," he pointed out angrily.

She was on her deathbed, she insisted, and she was not going to be dragged off of it for some silly superstition.

"Silly superstition?" Peppy sputtered. "What about the Evil Eye? Who was it that took me to Za Rose's house when I was ten to have the Malocchio lifted?!" He took a breath. "No! Never mind! You know what? We don't want you. Don't come! Just stay here and ruin everybody's Thanksgiving. Including your Grandchildren's!"

A sudden hush fell onto the room. Peppy had played the Grandchildren card, and while he held that momentary advantage he stomped out of the room, the pungent odor of VapoRub clinging to his clothes.

Dad and Peppy stood at the front door, deciding if they should drive together or if Dad should drive alone, when Mom's voice wavered down the stairs once more. "I'll come to your dinner," she said weakly, "but I'm doing it for the Grandchildren! You don't care about me at all." Peppy had won, but the victory had not come cheaply. The price of martyrdom was guilt, and Mom drove a bargain like a Turkish rug dealer.

Peppy returned to the club, and Mom and Dad followed shortly. Mom was dressed in a black dress—the one she normally wore to funerals—with a touch of rouge to highlight the fevered flush of each cheek. The odor of Heaven Scent now mingled with VapoRub in an unruly competition.

Mom greeted everyone with a hoarse whisper and a brave smile, and we all pushed up to the table. Peppy bowed his head to say Grace. He thanked the Lord for allowing the family to be together on this special day, and he was especially grateful, he said, that his mother was able to be with us in spite of her illness. He glanced up before he pronounced Amen, and he saw that every head was bowed except Mom's, who was glaring across the table at him.

All through dinner Mom refused to eat a bite, and as soon as desert was served, she excused herself, saying that she really did feel quite poorly. Peppy followed her from the table as she left the room.

"I'm sorry Mom," he said, as he helped her into her coat. "I love you, you know."

"I know," she said, "and I hope you're satisfied. The things I do for my ungrateful son," and she kissed him. "The turkey looked a little dry," she said as she turned and walked away.

Meanwhile, Dale and I, back at the table, were completely unaware of the family drama that had played out that day. It would be many years before I was told the full story and learned that the presence of Steve at so many functions had been to fill out a table and avoid the curse of the Last Supper.

When Peppy returned from the coat room, Dale and I were still sitting over our deserts. "I'm glad everything worked out today," Dale said as Peppy walked up. "I know I showed up last minute, and Al's jacket was a little tight, but after we got here, I didn't have to wear it," he shrugged, "so it turns out it was no big deal."

Peppy sat down heavily and fixed Dale with a stare that caused chills to run down my spine. Silly superstition or not, I suddenly felt the urge to take Dale straight to Za Rose's house.

Peppy with Mom. After they made up.

Now Bring Us a Figgy Pudding or an Old Style

We spent five years in our little townhouse in Frankfort Square, working hard at growing the dental practice and saving our money before building a new house and moving into Frankfort proper. The Butternut subdivision was recently carved out of a wooded area on the north side of Frankfort, and in November, when we moved in, we were one of nine families newly settled onto a cul-de-sac.

By mid-December we were mostly unpacked, and we decided to host a house-warming party. The invitation cautioned everyone to dress warmly, because it was the Christmas season, and we were going to go caroling.

Our guests began to arrive in the early evening, and we mingled in the house, practicing songs around the piano and drinking eggnog spiked liberally with brandy. After we had fortified ourselves with enough eggnog, we put on our coats and trooped next door to begin our caroling at the Krusemark house.

Al and Lyn Krusemark were newly married, and Lyn answered the door in her robe and pajamas, while Al looked over his shoulder from the sofa. They were both suffering from head colds, and they obviously had plans to watch a little television and call it an early evening. But they came to the door and graciously listened while we sang *Silent Night* and *Grandma Got Run Over by a Reindeer.* Lyn even offered to serve us cookies and cocoa, but we begged off. She was sick, remember, and nobody wants cookies or cocoa served by a sick person.

As we were turning from their doorway, another car pulled onto the crowded street, and two late arrivals, Mark and Marilyn, climbed out. "Your timing's perfect!" I called. "We were just leaving to go caroling. Come with us."

"No," Mark said. "I'm not much of a singer, and it's cold out. Marilyn and I will just wait in the house for you to come back."

"Ok, suit yourselves," I said. "The front door is open. Help yourselves to whatever you want. There's beer in the fridge." And with that, the rest of us continued on. Out of the driveway and down the street without a backward glance.

Mark and Marilyn watched us go, then turned, walked down the driveway, opened the door, and walked in without ringing the bell. Al and Lyn looked up from the couch in surprise as two complete strangers walked through their front door without knocking.

"Merry Christmas!" Mark called out as he waved a hand in their direction. "Don't get up. I'm going to grab a beer out of the fridge." He pointed down the hall toward the kitchen. "In here?" Al nodded dumbly and looked at Lyn in amazement.

Home invaders! Their home was apparently being burgled, in front of their very eyes, by a well-dressed couple who were going to start with the beer from their fridge! Unbelievable, and yet...

Suddenly, an explanation occurred to both Al and Lyn at the same moment. As newlyweds, they each assumed that these strangers were relatives of the other. The eccentric cousins that the rest of the family didn't talk about and whom they were meeting now for the first time.

Mark walked into the kitchen and began to rummage through the refrigerator. "There's only light beer," he called. "Do you think there's any Old Style someplace?" Lyn glared at Al as she heaved herself off the sofa and went into the kitchen to help Mark find a beer. Marilyn was settled onto the couch watching TV with Al, and Mark had finished his beer before the truth slowly untangled itself, and they were mercifully directed next door.

The Krusemarks later sold their home and moved away. Oddly, they didn't leave the subdivision. They built another house in Butternut. They just, moved away. I always thought that was strange.

Good Neighbors

Good neighbors are a blessing, I've been told, and I try my best to be one. I don't go outside in my underwear to pick up the morning paper, for example, and if I have to use the bathroom, I usually come inside to do it. But it may have been Confucius who said, "Good fences make good neighbors," and our Homeowner's Association didn't allow fences.

When we moved into our new home, we met the neighbors, not all at once, but in a series of small skirmishes. Most of us were young. Some had children. We were all busy. Many of us moved in at about the same time, over the fall and winter of '86, and we mostly met for the first time as we emerged from our homes, like bears from caves, as the days warmed in the spring.

The neighbor to the rear of our house introduced himself one warm spring day as I was cutting a walking trail through the wooded easement that fills our lot along its back edge. I had been working my chainsaw for almost a half hour when he materialized through the blue fog of exhaust. I pressed the kill switch and in the sudden silence wiped a hand on my jeans and stuck it out in greeting.

"Hi," I said. "My name's Al. I own the house right over there."

"Hi, Al," he said cautiously. "What are you doing?"

"I'm cutting out some brush and deadwood to make a walking path through the woods here," I answered proudly.

"Cutting out brush and deadwood, eh?" he said doubtfully. "You know you're on my property?"

Well, no, I hadn't known that. Apparently, I had generously overestimated the extent of my property at the rear of my lot, and I was laying waste to the vegetation of his back yard. It turns out that the pie shaped lot described to you by your realtor does not imply a curved crust. Rather, the back edge of your pie is a straight line that comes significantly closer to your house in the middle than you might have thought. I mean, it's a *triangular* shaped lot, all right? Let's not make references to a pie, and perhaps we can all avoid these embarrassments in the future.

The next morning my neighbor had tied bright yellow ribbons of plastic to the trunk of every tree along the boundary between our lots. After that, my neighbor to the rear dealt with me mostly by avoidance, coming to visit only on the occasions that I fogged my backyard for mosquitoes and the fumes settled onto his deck and inspired him to drop by with a pocket handkerchief held over his nose and mouth. But the Krusemark family next door was less fortunate.

There was a deep ditch which separated our properties, and I, being mostly hillbilly in my upbringing, used this ditch to dispose of my raked leaves. Every so often, I dealt with the accumulation of leaves by setting fire to them. Several years after we moved in, I decided it was time to do a controlled burn of my ditch. And by controlled burn, I mean one where I unrolled the garden hose before I lit the fire.

There are many ways to light a fire, and on the farm, we use gasoline. It gets the job done in a hurry, and farmers are busy people, without a lot of time to waste watching a fire smolder. I laid out the garden hose and dug out a book of matches, then I went into the garage and came out with a red gallon container. I sloshed gasoline generously over the accumulated leaves, using up most of the gallon. I carefully set the remainder of the gallon aside before I pulled a match from the book, but just then, as I stood poised to strike the match, Lyn Krusemark pulled into her driveway and climbed out of her car, towing her three small daughters. I waited, match in hand, as she walked onto my driveway.

"Hi, Al," she called brightly. "What are you doing?"

"I'm going to burn off the leaves in the ditch," I answered.

Lyn eyed the red can sitting just inside the garage suspiciously and sniffed delicately at the air. "Are you using gasoline?" she asked. "Isn't that dangerous?"

"Well, it could be," I said. "You have to know what you're doing." And with that, I cautioned her to stand back, struck a match, and tossed it in the direction of the gasoline-soaked leaves. The match settled lightly onto the leaves as Lyn pushed the girls behind her, and we both took a step back. For a moment nothing happened, and then the topmost leaf caught fire and began to burn with a merry flame. We walked forward and leaned over the edge of the ditch.

"There you go," I said smugly.

And then, as if to punctuate my words, the entire ditch exploded. Burning leaves rose into the sky on the winds of hell-fire and covered the majority of a half-acre, but mostly they settled onto the Krusemarks' cedar shake roof. Lyn, with a child clutched under each arm and one apparently held in her teeth, simply disappeared into her house, which struck me as irresponsible, given that her house was the second most likely thing in the neighborhood to be on fire, after the ditch itself.

I grabbed the hose and began to pour water onto as much of the Krusemarks' roof as I could reach.

What had happened, of course, was obvious in hindsight. While Lyn and I stood talking, the gasoline fumes, heavier than air and very explosive, had settled into the bottom of the ditch, and when I finally threw the match, the result, while not immediate, was spectacular.

So, you see, it wasn't entirely my fault. Lynn, with her neighborly chit chat, had interrupted my workflow, and was partially responsible. I suspected, however, as I began to get the flames under control, that I was likely to be assigned a disproportionate share of the blame.

After I put away the hose, I went back into the house where I found my phone already ringing. "Al," Lyn began without taking the trouble to introduce herself, "I don't think you should burn that ditch with gasoline anymore."

"Well, you may be right," I admitted quietly.

I didn't bring up the issue of sharing the blame, because, after all, I try to be a good neighbor.

Leaves of Three

Our home in Butternut was set into a wooded landscape of verdant green. Huge oak trees majestically spread their limbs throughout the neighborhood, and our lot was fringed by an easement along the rear that featured elms, ash, and maples. I cut a walking path through the tangled undergrowth and set about improving on Mother nature's design by planting a variety of wildflowers to add color to the mix.

And that is how I became the Poison Ivy Authority in Frankfort.

Oddly, having grown up on a farm, where I had an intimate relationship with vegetation of many varieties, including an assortment of itchy nettles and poisonous plants, I had never seen poison ivy. Apparently, it didn't exist in northwestern Illinois, and I had no idea what it looked like, other than that it had "leaves of three."

My first encounter, then, came on an unseasonably warm day in the spring of '87 while planting daylilies along the edge of my lawn where it bordered the naturalized easement. My mother had given me the daylily bulbs, which she had dug from the hillside in front of the old farmhouse where they bloomed each year in an explosion of orange. I was digging with a small hand-trowel, grabbing great handfuls of leafy vegetation and ripping it out by its roots. Long, trailing vines often had me pulling hand over hand and gathering them in against my chest before tossing them onto a growing pile at my side. I was dressed in shorts and a tee shirt, but as the sun warmed my back, I pulled off the shirt. Sweat ran down my bare chest, and I wiped it away with a green stained hand. I knelt in the dirt for an hour, ripping vines out of the soil and planting bulbs, and when I finished, I cleaned my tools, went inside, and washed my hands and face.

It was a day later that I noticed a small red bump on my chest. It was soon joined by several more, and when my outbreak was complete, I was one massive oozing sore. My arms. My chest. My stomach. From my belt to my neck. Each leg from the cuff of my shorts to my ankles. I looked like the Elephant Man, or what the Elephant Man would have looked like if he had had a really bad case of poison ivy instead of whatever disfiguring disease he actually had.

I lathered myself in Calamine lotion and went to work wearing long sleeved shirts and smelling like a pharmacy. My only relief came at night when I was able to stand under a scalding shower and let the water beat onto my raw chest until my body was numb.

Thus began my personal vendetta against poison ivy. In my mind, it became the Domestic Terrorist of weeds, and I vowed to exterminate it from my yard. For several years, I sprayed every three-leafed plant I saw at the edge of my lawn, but each year they returned in undiminished numbers. Finally, one spring, as I stood staring at my backyard and pondering the futility of my efforts, my eye was caught by the foliage of the tree shading my head. I looked up into the branches of a mid-sized tree and saw drooping leaves in groupings of three. It looked disturbingly like poison ivy, but it was a tree, with each leaf the size of my hand, and clusters of white berries hanging from each limb. I followed the branches to the main body of the tree and down the trunk. What I was looking at, what I was standing under, was a free-standing poison ivy tree! It had undoubtedly started its life as a small vine climbing the trunk of a nearby tree, but, over the years, it had grown, and the tree had died. And it had just kept on growing.

I had discovered the Mother Ship. From this tree, vines were crawling outward in all directions, and seeds were dropping and being scattered by birds. The focus of my campaign had found a new target. It was clear that in order to rid my yard of Ivy, I had to carry the battle onto the enemy's home world. Taking my assault into the depths of the forest, I cut down that tree with a hand saw and sprayed the stump with Ortho Poison Ivy Killer, my weapon of choice.

Now, you might think that as I entered the misty forest of my backyard and walked amidst the poison ivy, that I would have wrapped myself in layers of protective clothing, perhaps even using duct tape to seal the cuffs of my trousers. But no. This was no longer just a plant to me. This was the Enemy and deserving of my respect. We were entering into a battle from which only one would emerge, and I felt an odd compulsion to make the contest an even one. I stripped nearly naked as I went into the woods.

I walked slowly, like a man in a minefield, looking carefully before I placed each footstep. When I saw an ivy plant, I froze, one foot suspended in the air. I let my breathing slow and my eyes go unfocused, and soon I saw them all around. There was never a single plant. Poison ivy grows in clusters. And I sprayed them all. At night, as I lay in bed, I saw them again. Drooping, bright green leaves of three projected against my closed eyelids.

I found several more Mother Ships that first year. None was as big as the first, and none was free-standing, but each had a vine as thick as my wrist. When I cut them at their base, the entire tree that supported them wilted to brown. The only living thing up there having been poison ivy.

It took me five years, but each year there were fewer plants, until finally the day arrived when I found not a one. Call it VI Day. It was a glorious day. There weren't banner headlines or ticker-tape parades, but somewhere in New York City a man in uniform grabbed a woman, bent her back, and kissed her on the mouth.

I later cleared the poison ivy from the lot next to ours, as well. The Rossetto family had bought the Krusemark house shortly after the episode of the burning ditch, and Patty Rossetto, as it turned out, was sensitive to poison ivy. Whenever she was exposed to it, nothing more intimate than a handshake was exchanged in their house for nearly three weeks. I could have named my price when they called and asked for my help.

I didn't charge them a penny though, because poison ivy is my natural enemy. Its very existence is an affront to my sense of an ordered universe, and, like Batman to the Bat Signal, I answer the call whenever it comes.

So, if you need help with your poison ivy, raise the Bat Signal, and I will respond.

Remember to pull your blinds though, because I'm coming over naked.

With me, it's personal.

A New Charm

Cindy stretched her wrist across the table and dangled it in front of her mother. She was wearing a charm bracelet that her parents had given her as a child. On it were golden charms set with colored gemstones that marked the milestones of her life. There was a tiny bouquet of roses that represented her introduction as a debutant at her "Pink Bud" ceremony. There was a small golden diploma that celebrated her graduation from high school as class valedictorian, and wedding bells whose clappers were small diamonds that symbolized our wedding.

And now, as she jingled it in front of her mother, there was a tiny golden pacifier.

"Oh," her mom said, "you're wearing your charm bracelet. How beautiful."

Cindy gave the pacifier a flick. "Notice anything new?" she asked.

Cindy's mother looked more closely. "Is this a new one? A pacifier? What does that mean? Are you..."

Cindy was pregnant.

We had been married now for twelve years, and during that time I had gone to dental school, Cindy had gotten her MBA at the University of Chicago and her CPA immediately after, we had moved four times and built a house, we had started and grown my dental practice while Cindy had risen to Vice President with the Inland Steel Company, and we had answered the question, "When are you going to make us Grandparents?" countless times.

The questioning had gone from occasional, during the first three years of our marriage, to incessant during the following three, to occasional again, and finally to an uncomfortable silence that had fallen over the subject for the past several years. Tears now flowed from Cindy's mother's eyes, and her dad blotted his own with a pocket handkerchief. "We thought you couldn't have children!" her mom sobbed. "We thought there was something wrong with Alan that you didn't want to tell us." I sat up straighter in my chair with an insulted look on my face. "But now you're pregnant? You're going to have a baby?" and Cindy's mother dissolved into a small puddle of Italian Mother-in-law happiness.

I had friends from high school who, at my same age, were grandparents. Their first child had been born when they themselves were seventeen, and I admired their courage, if that's what it was. Because as I sat here now, thirty-four years old, I felt anything but ready to take on the responsibility of raising a child. If I had gone to a shelter and tried to adopt a dog, they would have put me through a screening process to determine if I were capable of providing a good home for the dog, and there was a better than even chance that I would have gone home without one. But everyone was just fine, apparently, with me taking immediate and untrained responsibility for raising a human child.

But the process had been begun, and there was no turning back.

Cindy's pregnancy progressed smoothly. There came a day when she gave a sudden gasp, and said, "The baby just moved. Come put your hand here and feel." So I did, but I felt nothing. I knew there was a baby in there, but I was really taking Cindy's word for it.

Women are fully conscious of the new life growing within them. They feel the baby hic-cup and turn. They have morning sickness and the constant urge to pee. Their feet grow a size and a half. But men have to take their word for it. We see the belly grow, and eventually we do feel the baby move, but its more of an abstraction for us. Its like the women were *there* at Pearl Harbor, and we saw the movie.

Cindy's was a summer pregnancy, and the summer of 1988 set a record for the most days with a temperature exceeding one hundred degrees. Cindy lay in bed at night on top of the covers with the ceiling fan on turbo and the air conditioning set to Meat Locker, and she tossed restlessly and repeated endlessly, "It's hot in here. Are you hot? It is so *hot* in here," while I lay curled under an electric blanket turned as high as it would go.

Finally, the day arrived when Cindy went into labor. She was two weeks overdue, and those two weeks hadn't been pleasant. Doctors confidently give young couples a due date at their first pre-natal visit, and the expectant parents latch onto that date as if Moses handed it to them on a stone tablet. "Your due date is September 1," Dr Bush had said. So, we set our mental clocks for September 1. We committed to that time span, but when September 1 came and went, Dr. Bush was officially in breach of contract. By the time Cindy's labor began on the fourteenth, we were considering legal action.

There's a book called *What to Expect when You're Expecting* that every pregnant couple reads. Cindy read it, and I was supposed to, but when I did, I treated it like my neuro anatomy textbook during dental school. There was valuable information in both books, I'm sure, but since it didn't apply directly to me, I skimmed it.

When Cindy went into labor then, I was less prepared than I might have been. I timed her contractions, which was one of my duties as outlined by our Lamaze instructor, and Cindy assured me that she was fine. These were early contractions, she said, and it would be a while before things got serious. I paced nervously through the house between contractions, convinced that Cindy was taking this process too lightly. Things were not progressing as quickly as they should, I thought, or perhaps they were further along than we realized. In either case we should be on our way to the hospital.

It was at this moment, with my psyche in that fragile state, that we lost power in the house. I hadn't even been aware of the storm building outside, but as the house went dark my courage broke. I simply could not sit in a dark house on a stormy night, using a flashlight to time contractions for my delusional wife. I bundled her into the car, and we drove through the storm to the hospital.

There they carefully examined Cindy and pronounced her fit and well. She was in early labor, they said, and we should go home and return when her labor had progressed. I may have caused a scene. I really don't recall. I think I cried a little. "Don't make us go back home," I pleaded. "It's dark there, and I don't think I can do this at home, alone, in the dark."

They pointed out that this was not about me, but they finally gave in to my shameless begging and tucked Cindy into an out of the way room, where I could time her contractions surrounded by the comfort and security of a fully staffed medical facility ready to intervene should anything burst or go sideways.

We were there for the next thirty-six hours, and Cindy gradually came around to my way of thinking. Her labor was not following the course outlined in the book.

Dr. Bush finally came into the room, and, with a concerned scowl, told us that the baby was starting to show signs of distress, and Cindy needed to go for an emergency C-section. It was two in the morning on the sixteenth at this point, and an anesthesiologist was dragged from his bed to do a spinal injection. The first injection didn't provide full anesthesia, so they sat Cindy up and gave her a second shot. I was ushered back into the room, gowned and masked, and squeezed in at the top of the table with the anesthesiologist and Cindy's draped head. Her body was mostly hidden behind a large blue screen where Dr. Bush and his assistant were already at work.

During my year as a Resident at Michael Reese hospital, I had spent two months doing a rotation in anesthesia, so I looked around the room now and surveyed all the various instruments with a feeling of familiarity. My attention was finally drawn back to Cindy as she whispered something I didn't quite hear. "Icn br," she said faintly.

"What?" I asked, leaning closer.

There was a pause, so long that I had gone back to looking around the room, before she repeated, "I cn br!"

I looked up at the anesthesiologist who was busily checking his monitors and IV flows. "I think she just said she can't breathe," I said.

He looked down at Cindy. "Oh no, no," he said with a heavy accent. "If she could not breath, she could not speak." And he returned to his interrupted tasks.

I looked back at Cindy, who's eyes were pleading with me, and, after a longer pause, she whispered again, "Icn brth." I turned back to the anesthesiologist. "Ok," I said firmly, "but how about you and I pretend like she can't breathe, and you grab an Ambu bag and breath for her."

He must have dealt with hysterical fathers before, because after a quick look into my eyes, to his credit, he reached for an Ambu bag and began to give Cindy slow deep breaths.

Meanwhile, Dr. Bush was busily pulling body parts out from inside of Cindy and lying them onto the surgical draping. I'm not sure what they all were, but I assume there was a reason they had to come out, and when he was finished, he put them all back in. Then there was a moment of tense expectancy in the room, and Dr. Bush raised a squalling baby girl into the air. She was perfect in every way, except for a mysterious coating of green that covered her from head to toe. Dr. Bush explained that this was meconium, which turned out to be a polite word for pre-natal baby poop, and it was a result of her having been two weeks overdue. We're fortunate, I suppose, that the Health department hadn't come in and shut us down for sanitary violations.

After they cleaned her up and moved Cindy back into her room, they brought her in and laid her into Cindy's arms. I sat beside her and looked at our baby girl for the first time. In the delivery room, I had been too concerned about Cindy's distress and the greenness of the baby to have really focused properly. Now, as I looked at her lying in Cindy's arms and then held her myself, I found myself overwhelmed with love for this tiny creature. It was amazing. Shocking. Breathtaking, really. It was the most powerful emotion I have ever felt. This baby had done nothing yet to deserve my love, and yet I was suffused in a glow of total rapture.

There was a lot of ancient chemistry involved in that moment, I know. In our evolutionary past, if parents hadn't felt this overwhelming surge of love for their offspring, they might very well have eaten them. But that knowledge, that I was at the mercy of a flood of prehistoric hormones, didn't detract in any way from my experience. I loved that little girl more than I had ever loved anything, and when, two years later, my son was born, I loved him the same. Thirty years have passed, and the hormone rush has worn off, but my feelings for my children remain the same. I would have to be really, *really* hungry before I would consider eating either one of them.

Cindy's charm bracelet gained a pacifier for Corielle and a clown for Tony.

My two favorite children. Corielle – age two, and Tony – newborn

Because That's What Friends Do

If you've ever built a house, or remodeled a kitchen, you know the agony and the angst that accompany it. The process wears away at you. It beats you down. And it's not the big things that do the wearing and the beating, it's the little ones. There are thousands of details to be dealt with. None are earth-shaking, but they are all decisions that have to be made, and they pile up until finally you're pulling your hair out and announcing to anyone who'll listen that all you really want are four walls and a roof.

That's when you need a friend to calm you down, to put a hand on your shoulder and tell you everything will be all right, because that's what friends do for one another.

It was eleven o'clock at night when my doorbell rang, and I found Bill Holley standing distractedly on the stoop. Bill was one of our best and oldest Frankfort friends. He and his wife Linda had lived in the townhouse which adjoined ours in Frankfort Square, and, for the past several years, they had owned a home just down the street from us. Now, as it happened, they were in the final weeks of building a new house in another subdivision in Frankfort, and the strain was beginning to tell.

"Al," Bill said without preamble, "I need to look at your ironing board."

He pushed past me and hurried up the steps and into the laundry room without waiting for an answer. After a few minutes spent silently studying my fold-down ironing board, he mumbled his thanks and disappeared as quickly as he'd come.

I looked at Cindy with raised eyebrows. "He's losing it." I said.

The very next day, as luck would have it, found the Building Inspector for the Village of Frankfort sitting in my dental chair. "Tom," I said slowly, as an idea began to take shape, "how would an average person, such as myself, get their hands on one of those stickers the Village puts up when a construction project is out of compliance?"

"Stop Work stickers?" Tom asked. "I have some in the truck. What do you want one for?"

"A friend needs our help," I answered.

The plan that came together over the next several minutes was the work of genius. First, a Stop Work order would be placed in the front window of Bill's new house. Tom would handle this. A short time later I would take Bill out to the house and let him discover the sign. Bill would, of course, wonder what the problem was, and I would tell him that I knew the Building Inspector, and with a simple phone call we could put the matter right. Next, we would call Tom, who would drive out to the site and tell Bill that his house had been built two feet too close to the property line and would have to be moved.

"It's not your fault," Tom would say. "It should have been caught at the survey, but it wasn't, and now the house has to be moved over two feet, that's all." Bill would fume and tear his hair and probably insist that homes were not something one casually moved over two feet, and Tom and I would reach into our pockets, pull out novelty glasses with fake noses and bushy black eyebrows, put them on, and simply stare at Bill until he caught on.

I called Pat O'Donnell, Bill's General Contractor, to let him in on the plan so he wouldn't be caught unawares when a Stop Work order appeared at his job site. "Ah, tha'll be a fine joke on Mr. 'Olley," Pat declared in his broad Irish brogue.

The plan was military in its precision. The clock would start when Tom put up the Stop Work order as he left work at three thirty. At five o'clock sharp I would pick Bill up and drive him over to the house on an invented pretext. At five thirty we would call Tom at home. He would come over to the house, and by six o'clock we would all be wearing novelty glasses and laughing.

That was the plan, and it started to go wrong almost immediately.

At three thirty I walked past Bill's old house and found him about to drive out to the construction site. The sign would already be in place, but it was still T minus ninety minutes to Practical Joke lift-off. This was going to put the entire plan badly off schedule. I had no choice but to join Bill in the car and adapt on the fly. As we pulled into Bill's driveway, the construction foreman was standing in the front doorway holding a hammer. He was a small Irish fellow who looked at us with an unreadable expression. Clearly visible on the window to his right was a bright red sign that read "Stop Work."

"What's that?" Bill called to the foreman as he pointed to the sign.

"Well," said the foreman as he slipped his hammer into its belt loop, "Ah don' exactly know. A man from ta village was 'ere not 'alf an hour ago, and he said the 'ouse was built two feet too close to the property line and would 'av to be moved. All I know for sure is tha' na another lick o' work can be doon until tha's taken care of."

I was in awe. He had done it beautifully. He hadn't batted an eye or changed expression. Even I believed him.

"What?!" Bill sputtered. "Too close to the property line? How can that be? You can't move a house!"

"Well," said the foreman as he packed away his tools, "you could go to ta village and ask aboot a variance I suppose."

Bill looked up hopefully. "A variance?" he asked. "How long would that take? We move in two weeks."

"Oh no, I do na' think so," the foreman chuckled. "Those things take moonths and moonths. You'll be better off movin' the 'ouse."

Bill turned on his heel and stomped back to the car.

By the time I slid into the passenger seat he had his cell phone out and was punching in a number. "My sister-in-law's an attorney." he said through clenched teeth. "We'll see what she has to say about this! "

"I know the Building Inspector," I interjected weakly, trying to get back on script, "maybe we can..." Bill stopped me by holding up a finger. "Hi," he said into the phone, "it's Bill. We've got an issue with the house."

After a short conversation, it was established that nothing could be done until the next day, and Bill hung up the phone. We were way off book by now, but I still had hopes of salvaging the situation. "This is ridiculous," I said. "I know the building inspector. Let's give him a call and see if we can't get him out here and get to the bottom of this thing." I took Bill's phone and called the village, only to find that Tom had indeed left for the day, and I knew from our planning that he was now unavailable until five thirty. "He's gone home," I told Bill as I handed back the phone, "but we can get hold of him later, and I'm sure we can figure this out."

By this time, we were back at Bill's old house, and he was digging through paperwork for Pat O'Donnell's phone number. "Pat?" he said, "Bill Holley here. Hey, I was just out at the house and there's a Stop Work order on my window!"

By leaning closer, I could make out Pat's voice.

"Ah, Mr. 'Olley," he answered, "I 'eard aboot tha'. It's too bad, really. The 'ouse is set two feet too close to the property line they say, but doon you worry, tha'll na' be a problem. I can cut tha' two feet off your garage and use the lumber to build a play 'ouse in the back yard for the kiddies."

Again, I was in awe. Apparently, every Irishman has kissed the Blarney Stone at least twice.

Bill slammed down the receiver.

I eventually managed to calm Bill and assure him that at five thirty, when the Building Inspector was available, we would go back out to the house and get the whole thing straightened out. Moments later, as I walked home, I felt I finally had everything back under control. Not long after I got home, though, the phone rang. It was Mary Ellen Burfield, who lived next door to Bill.

"Al," she began, in a hesitant voice, "I hate to butt in, but I know you're friends with Bill, and I think he needs help. I can hear him from my house, yelling and cursing, and he's throwing furniture out of the house onto the driveway. Linda's taken the kids across the street, and they look really scared. I don't know what's wrong, but could you go over there and talk to him?" Apparently Bill was taking this harder than I had expected. I hung up on Mary Ellen and punched in Tom's number.

"Bill's not going to make it Tom," I said. "He's melting down. We need to do this now." But Tom was tied up at home, and five thirty was the absolute earliest he could get away. "All right," I sighed. "I'll try to hold him together until then."

I cut across the back yard and was at Bill's house in three minutes. Mary Ellen peeped out at me through the parted curtains of her living room window. Linda and the kids were huddled across the street on the curb. The Holley's driveway was cluttered with furniture, clothes, and toys. Strewn about in mute testimony to Bill's dementia. I knocked lightly on the door and walked into the house without waiting for an answer. I found Bill sitting at the kitchen table, his back toward me, hunched over the phone.

"I don't think I can go on," he sobbed into the receiver. "Everything has just gone to hell! We can't move in. And the house has to be *moved two feet*, for God's sake. And… I just don't think I can go on anymore!" The phone dropped from Bill's nerveless fingers and he fell forward, his body shaking with sobs as he buried his face in his arms.

My resolve finally broke. As much as I hated to give up on a joke, I couldn't go through with it while Bill sat sobbing at his kitchen table, apparently considering suicide. I picked up the receiver and dropped it into its cradle. "Bill," I began, "I'm sorry. This was all just a practical joke. Your house isn't too close to the property line. Everything's going to be all right," and I laid my hand gently on his shoulder.

The sobbing stopped immediately, and Bill lifted his head to look at me over his shoulder with suddenly dry eyes. He was wearing novelty glasses.

I stood, uncomprehending for several heartbeats as this awful turn of events seeped its way into my consciousness. Out of the corner of my eye I saw movement by the door, and I turned to see Mary Ellen, Linda, and the kids peeping gleefully into the room. I looked back at Bill, who now sat, smiling contentedly, where only moments before had been a man on the verge of taking his own life.

"No you didn't!" I shouted, as if the words were being torn from my mouth. "You did not know! I had you! Who… who… how?" I stuttered to a halt as I tried to compose my thoughts.

"I didn't know at first," Bill admitted with cruel amusement, "but I found out, and now the joke's on you."

Someone had broken. Someone had violated the Man Code. Someone, between the time I left Bill and when Mary Ellen called, had spilled the beans. I blamed so many people, then and over the years since. I confess to thinking it was Cindy for some time. She had hated the idea of the practical joke from the very beginning, and she could have called Bill, but she denied it, and I eventually came to believe her.

It has taken me years of contemplation and study, but this is what I believe happened. After I left Bill at his house, he again called Pat O'Donnell, this time threatening legal action, and Pat decided that things had gone far enough. A practical joke between friends was well and good, but this was business. And so he said, "Mr. 'Olley, your friend Al is 'avin' you on. It's all a practical joke don't you see. Your 'ouse is fine just where it is, and you'll be movin' in right on schedule."

I don't know this for a fact, though, because Bill won't tell me. Like Woodward and Bernstein, his source is a tightly held secret. But we have sworn an oath. Whichever of us passes away first, on the deathbed there will be a confession, because we're friends, and that's what friends do for one another.

The Pygmy People of Lithuania

I'd like to think that I was a good father. I really would. In fact, I thought once that I might be, but things happen that take your measure, and I've found that I come up short.

It happened long ago, when my daughter Corielle was about four years old, and my son Tony was two. We had dropped Cindy's car off at a shop just outside of Frankfort for repairs, and from there Cindy, the kids, and I took my car and spent the day in Chicago Heights, visiting her parents. Later in the day, a phone call confirmed that her car was ready to be picked up, and that the keys would be left under the floor mat.

It was evening as we made the trip home, and Corielle fell asleep in the back seat during the drive. When we arrived at the repair shop, Cindy jumped out of the car, and the slam of the door woke Corielle. She sleepily called from her car seat in the back, "Where's Mommy?"

That was the moment that took my measure.

"Mommy's gone," I said. Which, in my defense, was literally true, I suppose.

"Gone?" Corielle said nervously. "Gone where?"

And this was when I found out I wasn't a good father.

"She's gone to Lithuania to visit the Pygmy People," I said.

God help me, I have no idea where that came from. It just popped out of my mouth.

"Lithuania?!" Corielle looked around wildly. "No she isn't! She's in the car behind us."

And a good father would have said, "Yes Honey, she's right behind us. She's driving the other car home." But not me.

No, I said, "Yes, she's driving that car to Lithuania. We're going to go straight at this corner, to go home, but Mommy's going to turn right to go to Lithuania." And I went straight, taking a round-about way home, and Cindy turned right, as I knew she would, to take the more direct route.

Corielle started to cry in earnest now. "I don't want Mommy to go to Lithuania! I want her to come home with us."

"Well, Honey," I said, "we can go out tomorrow and get a new Mommy. A better Mommy. Wouldn't you like a younger Mommy, maybe with blond hair?"

"No!" Corielle sobbed, "I want my Mommy!"

It took us only four minutes to make the drive home, and all the way I talked about how nice it was in Lithuania this time of year, and how much fun Cindy would be having with the tiny Pygmy People, and how tomorrow we'd go shopping to pick out a new Mommy. And Corielle wailed from the back seat.

I fully expected to see Cindy in the driveway when we got home, but as it turned out, she'd stopped for gas. Again, a good father would have relented, but I looked around with delight and announced, "See? She's gone to Lithuania to visit the Pygmy People!"

When Cindy pulled into the driveway moments later, she looked at me with disbelief as she held Corielle and listened to her tear-choked story. She hugged her and told her that Mommy would never ever leave her, and anyway they didn't have pygmies in Lithuania, and Daddy said *what* about a new blond mommy?

Taken all together, neither Corielle nor Cindy saw the humor in the incident. I was heartless, they said, and cruel, and not a good father at all. And yet, about a week later, I pulled into the driveway and found Corielle upset again, this time because Cindy had told her *I'd* gone to Lithuania to visit the Pygmy People. Apparently it was funnier that way.

Over the years, Mommy's trip to Lithuania has taken on a life of its own. Corielle is twenty-two years old this year, and if she were to enter the room right now and ask, "Where's Mom?" I could answer, without looking up, "Gone to Lithuania to visit the Pygmy People," and Corielle would roll her eyes and walk out of the room.

I'm really not a very good father.

Yes, Virginia

As parents, we all wrestle with the Santa Claus question, which is part of the larger "lying to our children" issue, and I know there are those of you who want no part of it.

"If we tell them there's a Santa Claus," I can hear you whine, "and then they find out later that there isn't, they'll never trust us again!"

Well, I don't worry about that, because, if there's one thing I hope I've taught my children over the years, it's that I'm not trustworthy. I *will* lie to them, and often for no better reason than for my own amusement.

When Corielle and Tony were six and four years old respectively, we took them on a family trip to Washington, D.C., and I know what you're thinking, "What a great place to visit with the little ones!" and you're right. Their favorite part of the trip was when we found a playground with monkey bars, and I'm sure one of those could have been found closer to home. But when Corielle was fourteen months old, Cindy and I dropped her off with Grandma and Grandpa Heath while we went to a Dental Convention in Hawaii. The entire time we were gone the days were filled with separation anxiety, potty-training regression, crying in the nighttime, and refusal to eat. That was Cindy. Corielle did fine. But after that Cindy insisted that we travel everywhere with the kids, and so we ended up in Washington, D.C. with two preschoolers.

We were walking through a park near the Capitol buildings, and I was several steps ahead of Cindy and the kids. I had my hands in my pockets jingling some loose change. I pulled out a nickel, a dime, and a few pennies, balanced the coins on the nail of my thumb, and, with a flick, sent them spinning into the overhanging branches of a tree. Tony and Corielle, following close behind, were pelted with coins raining down from an apparently empty tree.

"Hey," Corielle shouted, "money just fell out of this tree!"

I turned around and walked back. Looking up into the tree, I stroked my chin thoughtfully. "It's probably the squirrels," I said. "In Washington they have so much money that squirrels throw it out of the trees."

For the rest of the week I flipped coins into trees at every opportunity, and Tony and Corielle scrambled around like kids on an Easter egg hunt, collecting coins and searching for a glimpse of a philanthropic squirrel. Toward the end of the trip, Corielle approached a group of homeless men huddled around a fire set in a trash can. She handed one of them a handful of coins. "Here," she said. "You don't have to be hungry. Just go into the park. The squirrels are throwing money out of the trees."

Sometimes my lies were more altruistic.

Walking through Butternut one evening, we found a small bird lying broken on a neighbor's porch. It had flown into their large plate glass window and was obviously injured beyond healing. Having grown up on a farm, where life is cruel and sometimes short, I was in favor of ending its misery, but Corielle had other plans.

"We have to take it home and make it better," she declared.

I knew it wasn't right to let her get her hopes up, so I was firm. "No, Honey," I explained, "this bird is hurt too badly to get better. It will be kinder to end its suffering right now." So, after we got it home, we put it into a box, bedded into a nest of torn newspaper and sprinkled with birdseed. Corielle had decided that its name was Bird on the Wing, which was either hopeful or ironic, depending on your point of view.

"Good night, Bird on the Wing," she whispered as she pushed a pile of birdseed to within easy reach. "You eat and get better, and I'll see you tomorrow."

The next morning, when I went to check on Bird on the Wing, he lay exactly as we had left him; so tiny, so helpless, and now stiff and so unquestionably dead. My heart broke as I looked into the nest that Corielle had built, and I couldn't bear the thought of her seeing this pathetic ending. I gathered up Bird on the Wing's mortal remains and put them into the bottom of the garbage container in the garage. Then, when Corielle came downstairs, I was ready with a story.

"You wouldn't believe it," I said. "I came downstairs, and Bird on the Wing was out of his box and flying around the breezeway in circles. He was completely better. I suppose it was the birdseed that did it, but anyway, I opened the door and he just flew out! That's him over there," and I pointed to a random bird perched in the Ash tree by our front door.

Corielle squinted in the direction of the Ash. "I see him!" she squealed with delight. "Do you think he'll stay for awhile?"

"I would imagine he would," I answered. "After all, you saved his life."

Bird on the Wing lived in that tree outside our house for years. He migrated in the winter and returned every summer. We never had any trouble recognizing him either. He was every small brown bird in the Ash tree by the front door.

Which brings us at last to Santa Claus.

One Christmas, when Corielle was barely three, we had house guests for the holidays. Lee and Jeff Miller, whom we had met, incidentally, at that Dental Convention in Hawaii, came to spend several days with us, including Christmas Day, and Jeff arrived with a complete and authentic Santa suit packed in his luggage.

He had no actual plan regarding the suit prior to his arrival but having a Santa suit is like having a whoopee cushion. You don't know you need one until you have it, but once you have it, you feel compelled to use it. After Corielle had set out milk and cookies on Christmas eve, and she and Tony were tucked snuggly into bed, we sprang into action. Jeff dressed in the Santa suit while we filled a large laundry bag with the kid's gifts. The camcorder was set onto the dining room table, aimed so that it looked across the milk and cookies and took in the living room with the fireplace and the Christmas tree. We backed Jeff into the fireplace with the laundry bag slung over his shoulder and set the camera to "record." Moments later Jeff crawled into the room, to all appearances having just dropped down through the chimney.

"Ho, Ho, Ho!" Jeff chuckled. "Now, who do we have here?" and he consulted his list. "Well, now, Corielle and Tony. It says here they've both been very good boys and girls this year! Let's see what we have for them." He began to pull their gifts from his bag and arrange them under the tree. After setting out the last of the presents, he walked to the dining room table. "Oh! They even remembered to put out milk and cookies for Santa," he said with delight, and, as he stepped briefly out of view, we flipped the recorder off.

The next morning Jeff got up early, put the suit back on, and waited patiently for the kids to stir. When he heard the pitter-patter of tiny feet upstairs, he turned on the camcorder, stepped back into view, and sat down, dunking his first cookie into the glass of milk. Corielle came into the room at a run and was halfway to the tree before she spotted Santa Claus sitting at the table. She froze, like a deer in headlights.

"Uh oh," Jeff said, "It looks like you caught me. It must be later than I thought. Have you been a good girl this year, Corielle?" In response, Corielle fled back up the stairs and into our bedroom, where Cindy and I were putting on robes and slippers.

"Santa's still downstairs!" she exclaimed. "I saw him!"

"Oh, Honey," we said calmly, "no one ever catches Santa. He's been and gone long ago. He comes while you're asleep."

"No, he's down there now. He's eating cookies. He asked if I'd been good. *He knew my name!*"

"Ok, calm down," we said, as we gathered Tony from his crib. "You just imagined it. Come on now, let's go downstairs."

Jeff, of course, had slipped back to his bedroom, leaving the first floor deserted. Corielle stared at the empty chair in confusion, but soon lost interest and focused on unwrapping her gifts. After a few minutes we were joined by Lee and Jeff, both yawning and wearing their bathrobes, and it was nearly an hour before someone discovered the camcorder on the dining room table.

"Well, let's have a look then," I said, "and see what we've got."

We put the tape in the VCR and there it was—undeniable proof of Santa's existence. The entire videotape was a masterpiece. Beginning with Jeff crawling from the fireplace, through his placement of the gifts, to his discovery by Corielle. It was a piece of documentary evidence that couldn't be questioned. There were some issues with lighting, but nothing that couldn't be fixed in post-production.

With what we came to refer to as the Santa Tape, the legend of Santa Claus was settled in our house. Corielle was a true believer, and when any of the neighborhood kids questioned Santa's existence, they were invited for a viewing, and they left converted.

Eventually, of course, Corielle had to be disabused of her notion. It wouldn't do for her to enter high school still believing in Santa, so I sat her down one day. "Corielle," I said in a confidential whisper, "Mom and I want you to help us with Tony. You're grown up now, and you know Santa's make believe, but Tony's just little, and we don't want you to tell him."

Corielle looked at me for a long minute. "But what about the Santa Tape?" she asked.

"That was Uncle Jeff," I said.

"Oh," she said slowly, "I always thought he looked a little fakey."

That may have been a good time to discuss Bird on the Wing as well, but I left that for another day. I'd already had as much honesty as I could stand at one time.

A Mid-Life Rodeo

"Climb on up here Doc," Brian called out.

So I climbed on up.

"Now, straddle the fence," Brian said, "and let yourself down onto the horse easy, but be careful you don't touch her with your spurs."

Brian slapped my hand where I gripped the riggin'. "How do you feel?"

Honestly? I felt like I was about to do something really stupid.

Now, normally, when you're about to do something really stupid, you can't recall exactly how you came to be in that situation. Men often get a testosterone induced amnesia. But not in this case. No, I knew the exact moment that this all began.

I was waiting in line to pick up a fish dinner.

The "World Championship Rodeo" was coming to Frankfort, courtesy of the local VFW, and I was excited. I liked rodeos. The event was still a week away, and I was standing in line on a warm Friday night in September, waiting for my fish dinner at the VFW pavilion. Next to me was a poster, in garish yellow and red, featuring a photo of a cowboy riding a Brahma bull. I turned to Cheryl Howard, a friend who was joining us for dinner, and asked, nodding at the poster, "Are you going to the rodeo?"

Cheryl smirked an annoying smirk that is often smirked by people who think something is cruel or stupid. "No," she sniffed dismissively, "I don't think so."

My hackles rose at the tone of her voice. "Well, that's too bad," I said defensively, "because rodeos are fun. I just wish there were some way local people could ride in them, because I'd love to do that." I swear, I was just making conversation, filling the moment with idle chit-chat, but there are people in this world that you can say things like that in front of and get away with it, and Cheryl isn't one of them.

I picked up my plate and went to sit at an unoccupied picnic table. My fish hadn't cooled enough for my first bite when Cheryl reappeared with Big Bob Garrett, the VFW commander, in tow. "Hey Doc," Bob said, "Cheryl says you want to ride in the rodeo?"

I looked up with a startled, deer-in-the-headlights look. I saw Cheryl and knew in an instant what was going on, and I also knew that the next thing I should say was, "Are you crazy?" But when I looked over Bob's shoulder at Cheryl, who still had that smirk on her face, what came out of my mouth instead was, "Absolutely! Can I?"

"Shoot, anybody can ride in the rodeo," Bob said with mounting enthusiasm. "You just have to pay your entry fee, and get a Rodeo Rider's Union card, and buy some insurance. Anybody can ride! Jeez, I wish we'd known you wanted to do this, Al. We'd have put you into the advertising. People would come from all over to see a dentist ride in a rodeo. Hell, you could get hurt!"

Bob gave me a phone number to call the next Tuesday after one o'clock, and he walked away literally rubbing his hands together with glee at the prospect.

Tuesday came all too quickly, but when one o'clock rolled around, I pulled the phone number from my pocket and dialed. A cigarette-roughened female voice answered. "World Championship Rodeo, may help you?"

"Yes," I quavered, "Is this the place you sign up to ride in the rodeo?"

"Yes, it is. How may I help you?"

I decided to cut right to the chase. "Ok, so what do I do? I'd like to ride!"

The woman hesitated just briefly. "Ok, and what is your event?"

"Oh, I don't know," I said. "I guess Saddle Bronc."

The hesitation was longer this time. "And do you have a Professional Rodeo Rider's Union Card?" she asked.

"No," I admitted, "They told me I could get a temporary card for this event."

"That's true," she said slowly. "Do you have your own equipment?"

"I have boots," I answered proudly. "And I can borrow a hat. What else do I need?"

The woman had heard enough. "Sir," she intoned sternly, "you've never done this before have you?"

"Well, no." I admitted, "But I'm over forty, and I figure there're only so many ticks left on my clock before I can't do something like this anymore, and I don't want to pass up the opportunity."

She laughed, "Sir, if you're over forty, your clock has ticked."

I paused. "I'm going to need to talk to someone else," I said.

"All right," she said pleasantly, "but he's going to tell you the same thing."

And he did. "I'm sorry sir, but we get this all the time. Men of a certain age call up wanting to ride in a rodeo. We just can't allow it. Surely, you understand the risks?"

After I hung up, I was overwhelmed with relief. I had tried. And they wouldn't let me do it. I was off the hook, and it wasn't my fault. Another couple of days passed before Big Bob stuck his head into my office. He was putting up some last-minute posters, and he wondered how my entry was coming along.

"Sorry, Bob." I said dolefully. "They wouldn't let me do it. They said I was too old. I didn't have my own equipment. A lot of things. It just won't work out."

Bob's face fell. "That's too bad. Do you still want to do it?"

Now that the pressure was off, my machismo was back in full force. "Oh, yeh! I'm really disappointed."

"All right then, I'll see what I can do. When the guys come out to set up the rodeo grounds later today, I'll talk to them." And Bob turned and hurried away.

Crap! I had done it again.

Bob returned the next day.

"Hey Doc, how old are you?"

"Forty-one," I said.

"No, you're not," he said with a wink, "you're not quite thirty. And what kind of shape are you in?"

"Pretty good for forty-one," I said, "but not so hot, I suppose, for 'not quite thirty'."

"No," he said, "you're in great shape, and you ride all the time! I talked them into letting you ride Bareback Bronc!"

"Bob!" I said, with a horrified look, "I haven't been on a horse in years! And I wanted Saddle Bronc. I haven't ridden a horse bareback since I was a kid!"

"Nope," Bob called over his shoulder as he left the office, "Saddle Bronc's too dangerous. They said they'd let you go Bareback. Be there about one o'clock on Saturday."

That evening I dug out a roller blade wrist guard to wear on my right hand. If I broke my right wrist, I reasoned, I was out of work, and I couldn't have that. Then I headed to Action Sports to pick out a new athletic supporter, because I had other body parts I would just as soon weren't out of work either.

I rummaged through the display of athletic supporters for several minutes before I gave up and asked for help. "Excuse me," I whispered to the young girl behind the counter. "Where do you keep the adult sizes of athletic supporters?"

"There's none over there?" she asked.

"No," I said softly, "just youth sizes."

"Ok," she said. "HEY MA!" she shouted into the back of the store. "WHERE DO WE KEEP THE ADULT JOCK STRAPS?"

From the back, "WHAT SIZE?"

She, "What size?"

"I don't know, probably a medium. How do they come?" I hissed in my smallest voice.

She, "MEDIUM!"

"Could be a large," I amended.

The owner emerged from the back carrying a selection of supporters. "Oh, Al," she said. "What are you up to? Playing some football?"

"No," I said with a sheepish grin, "I'm riding in a rodeo tomorrow."

She looked at me silently for a minute, and then pushed the package across the counter. "This is on the house," she said softly.

The next day was Saturday, and my buddy Bill Holley picked me up after work. He had agreed to be my "corner man," and he proudly displayed the small first aid kit he had purchased for the occasion. It held several band-aids and a package of alcohol wipes. "Because you can't be too careful," he intoned seriously.

When we got to the VFW, a makeshift arena had been set up with bleachers on both sides and a corral holding the livestock at one end. Big Bob met us at the gate and took us to meet the rodeo manager. I stuck out my hand. "I understand I have to pay some fees and sign some papers?"

"Nope, no fees," he said. "We don't want you to pay no entry fee, and we don't want you to buy no insurance. You don't need to get a Union Card either. You're what we're going to call an exhibition rider, and you just need to sign this waiver that says you understand you could get killed and we're not responsible."

"Well," I swallowed, "I guess that sounds reasonable."

"Now, over there," he said, and he pointed to a young cowboy leaning against a trailer, "is Brian Massey. He's going to tell you what to do. Pay attention to what he says. He's the number three bareback money winner in the country so far this year, and he knows his stuff." He pushed a tattered leather and rope contraption into my hands. "This here is your riggin'," he said, "Brian will help you with that too."

Minutes later, Brian was looking me slowly up and down, as if I were some sort of curiosity that he had never encountered before. He spit a stream of tobacco juice, and finally looked me in the eye. "They say you're a dentist," he said. "That true?"

"Yeh," I admitted. "It is."

"Well, what the fuck you want to do this for?" he asked with sincere amazement.

"I don't know," I said honestly. "It sounded like a good idea at the time."

"Well," and he spit again, "pay attention, because I'm going to try to save your life. This here is your riggin'." And he took the straps from my hands. "We belt this around the horse, and you dig your hand into the handle and hold on for all you're worth. You hitch yourself right up over the handle with your hips, you lever your arm across your leg, and you squeeze for all you're worth. Every time the horse bucks, you reach out and hook with your spurs and pull with your legs for all you're worth." He paused and looked to see if he had my full attention. "Do you think you can remember all that?"

"I believe I can," I said.

"You got any questions?"

"Well, yes," I said. "You know how when the ride is over, and they come up beside you with that other horse to lift you off, so you don't have to jump? How do you do that?"

Brian looked at me in disbelief. "Shit," he said, "you don't have to worry about that!" And he turned and walked away.

In spite of Brian's lack of faith, I was feeling better than I had in days. Truth be told, I hadn't slept much since Thursday, and, as I lay awake in bed, trying to imagine how a person might stay on the back of a bucking bareback horse, I had come up with almost exactly what Brian had just told me. I suddenly felt that I might be all right.

Brian led me to the bullpen, where the other cowboys were stretching and warming up before their rides, and he pointed out a dappled gray mare in the livestock pen. "That's your horse," he said. "She's a good animal. She won't try to kill you."

I studied the other cowboys, and I did what they did. When they stretched, I stretched. When they spit, I spit. After a few minutes they ran the bareback horses from the holding pen into the individual loading chutes, and since my gray wasn't one of them, I went on stretching, not paying any particular attention now to the cowboys who were preparing to ride. Suddenly I heard a gate crash open, and I heard a noise that I didn't know a horse could make. It was an angry noise, filled with violence. Like a scream. And then clods of dirt started raining down into the bullpen.

I looked up as the horse pitched, spun, and launched its rider over its head and onto the ground. The horse continued to spin, and its hoof grazed the thrown rider's head. Men rushed out and lifted him to his feet and helped him from the arena. I will admit that I had held a mental image of my rodeo ride firmly in my head since I had first agreed to do it. It involved a horse that didn't scream. A horse that even liked me a little. One that gently bucked as it came out of the chute, and I would hold on, or I would fall off, but it was all civilized and gentle, and in the end, nobody got kicked in the head and was dragged, bleeding, from the arena.

What I had just seen was nothing like that. What I had just seen was dangerous. What I had just seen I could die doing. I felt like someone had poured ice-water down my back.

They released the next rider. He had my full attention this time. He slipped backwards onto the horse's rump and was launched fully ten feet into the air, finally coming to earth with an impact that I actually felt through my feet. His tail bone was the first thing to make contact with the ground, and he limped out of the arena under his own power, but only just.

Brian was next, and he too was thrown, crashing head foremost into the metal fencing that made up the arena's perimeter.

Bill, my corner man, appeared magically at my elbow. "Hey, Al," he said, with a concerned look on his face, "everybody sent me down here to talk you out of doing this. Are you still going through with it?"

I looked at him without recognition for a minute, and then, "Yeah, I guess I am."

He shook his head sadly. "You're up shit's creek!" he said, and he walked away, his obligations fulfilled.

The stands had gone quiet, or so it seemed to me. There were a lot of people here who had come to watch me ride, and the atmosphere had been party-like until the first rider went. A betting pool was being run, in fact, by the girls from my office. People drew numbers corresponding to how many seconds, to the nearest tenth, it would take before I was off the horse and in the dirt. But now, suddenly, it had occurred to them that they might all be out of work tomorrow.

Brian limped over to where I clung, white knuckled, to the fence. "Let's go Doc. Grab your riggin'" I noticed for the first time that they had run in the horses for the Saddle Bronc competition, and my gray was in the last chute. Oddly, that calmed my nerves. At least now I knew when I was to ride. At the end of all the bucking horse competition they were going to have their exhibition ride, and I would go last. I took a deep breath and gathered my riggin' from where it lay in the bullpen dirt.

Brian cinched it onto my horse while another young rider, the cowboy who had landed so hard on his tailbone, took off his spurs and offered them to me. "You can't ride without spurs," he said.

"Climb on up here, Doc." Brian called.

I climbed on up.

"Now straddle over across the fence and let yourself down easy onto the horse. Be careful you don't touch her with your spurs."

I slowly lowered myself onto the gray's back.

"Dig your hand into the handle like I told you!" Brian said sharply.

I dug in my hand.

Brian slapped at my hand. "All right now! Hitch yourself up over the handle like I told you!" Brian almost shouted. "Come on! How do you feel?"

"I feel fine," I said. Jesus, I thought, relax Brian. There are five horses yet to go before it's my turn. Let's chill out here a little.

"Ok!" Brian shouted, and he slapped again at my hand where I held loosely onto the riggin'. "When they open the chute, dig with your spurs! Now, how do you feel?!"

"I feel good," I said. And I did. I was relaxed and comfortable.

"Say when!" The voice came from behind me. I turned to look at a man holding an electric cattle prod poised over the flank of my horse.

"Now?" I quavered. I was really just asking. But the gate flew open and the man hit my horse with the electric prod. She whirled sideways and spun out into the arena, and as she whirled, she simply came out from underneath me.

You see, I wasn't gripping the handle for all I was worth. I wasn't levering my arm into my leg for all I was worth, and I wasn't digging with my spurs and pulling for all I was worth. It turns out that "for all you're worth" is very important, and I had failed to pick up on that part of Brian's speech earlier. As the horse left the chute, and I stayed behind, one thought filled my mind. After all this lead up, all this hubbub, my new jock strap, and all these people come to watch me ride, the horse was going to come out of the chute naked. The winner of the pool would be the guy who held "zero seconds," and I was going to dig a hole in the bullpen and pull the dirt in after me, because I was never going to hold my head up in town again.

But I hadn't come completely off. My left hand locked onto the handle and my left spur hooked the riggin'. As the horse finished her spin and took her first running buck, I was thrown into the air, and landed, miraculously, back on top of the horse. No one was more surprised than me. It took a second to realize that I was still horseback, but when I did, I gathered myself, reached with my spurs, dug, and pulled for all I was worth.

I was still on when the eight second horn blew, and I kicked off into the arena dirt. The crowd went wild! I was alive! And they were as relieved as I was.

I picked myself up, gathered my borrowed cowboy hat from where it had fallen, and used it to knock the dust off my pants. My body was awash with testosterone. You could have scraped it off my forehead and sold it to baseball players. I was an honest to God cowboy, and what was more, I was the only one to ride eight seconds that day. I threw my hat into the crowd, and it sailed into Cindy's outstretched hands. I walked out of the arena and back into the bullpen, my stride rolling on suddenly bowed legs.

Later, as Bill and I were leaving the emptying rodeo grounds, I saw the manager and went over to say goodbye. "I wanted to thank you again for letting me ride," I said. "I know you didn't want to at first, and I appreciate you making allowances."

"Oh, that's all right," he said. "You did good, Hoss. We didn't understand how it was at first. We thought you were older. You wouldn't believe how many guys over forty, you know, having a mid-life crisis, want to ride in a rodeo. We can't have that."

"No," I agreed, "you can't have that."

You can't tell from this photo, but I'm pulling for all I'm worth.

The Harsh Lens of Reality

There was a time, once, long ago, when I fancied that I struck an imposing figure. It wasn't true, of course, even then, and that was long ago, before I became old and wrinkled and not at all imposing. But once, long ago, there was a time.

It's a common enough delusion among men. Women view themselves through the harsh lens of cold reality. They look into a mirror and are horrified by what they see. Men, on the other hand, with their stomachs overhanging their belts like Poppin' Fresh biscuits and hair growing out of their ears and noses, will stare into a mirror, turn sideways, actually slap their protruding bellies, and enthuse, "I still got it!"

It takes a wake-up call to force us to look through that harsh lens that shows us as we truly are. My call came when I was working the concession stand at the Willow Valley Folk Festival one warm August day in 1995.

The Willow Folk Festival is an annual three-day music festival run by the Methodist Church that nestles in the valley below my parent's farm. A campground is established in a field across the gravel road from the church by the simple expedient of driving the cattle out of their pasture and setting up tents. A hay rack serves for a stage, and seating consists of wooden planks set onto hay bales. In the basement of the church, homemade pies and baked goods are sold by the Women's Club, and an outdoor concession stand is formed by a triangle of planks nailed between three enormous maple trees in the church yard.

The concession stand offers chips and candy bars, along with cans of pop cooled in a stock tank filled with fifty gallons of water and ice. It's run by the Methodist Youth Fellowship, and I, having been one of the original Methodist Youths at the Fest's inception in 1968, still put in time working the counter whenever I make it home for the Festival weekend.

I was working the last shift of the day with my brother-in-law Rich. The stage was quiet and empty, and the crowds were moving across the road to their campsites for the evening when I was suddenly overcome by a fit of whimsy. Now, I should explain that when I'm overcome by the whimsical fits, I'm no longer responsible for my actions. And so, when it struck me as an excellent idea to sneak up behind my brother-in-law, grab him around the waist, lift him into the air, and tip him headfirst into the tank filled with soda cans and ice water, it was done in an instant.

It was only after Rich rose from the water, like Godzilla from the swamps of New Jersey with ice cubes stuck in his hair, that I reevaluated the wisdom of my actions. Rich chased me for nearly five minutes before he collapsed against a tree, and stood, with his hands on his knees and his head hanging down, gasping for air and swearing loudly enough that I wasn't the only one who thought his behavior was inappropriate for a churchyard. After he regained his breath, he looked at me and said, quite seriously, "You know, you snuck up on me from behind there. In a regular wrestling match, I think I could take you."

I stared at him in disbelief.

Rich is fit enough, I suppose, but as far as I know the only athletic thing he has ever undertaken was a canoe trip, and that ended early when the floating cooler got away and all the beer was lost. "No, Rich," I said, in what I meant to be a kindly voice, "you couldn't."

"Yes," he insisted, "I think I could. I'm wiry."

"Wiry doesn't enter into it, Rich," I said. "It's like, if wrestling were a martial art, I would have a black belt. And you, well, you honestly wouldn't stand a chance."

I simply couldn't believe he was entertaining such a thought, but I couldn't talk him out of it, and we never got as far as having a wrestling match to settle the point. It was hot, and Rich was all wet and icky, so we eventually agreed to disagree and let the matter drop.

The following Monday I was back in the office telling this story to my assistant as we passed instruments back and forth across a patient. "Can believe that?" I asked. "He actually believed he could beat me in a wrestling match!"

Our patient mumbled something unintelligible through the wad of cotton stuffing his mouth.

"What?" I asked.

"Icd tku," he repeated.

I cleared his mouth of obstructions.

"What?" I asked again.

"I could take you," he said.

"What makes you say a thing like that?" I asked with a hysterical edge creeping into my voice.

"I'm strong, and I'm real quick," he said, and he raised one arm from the chair to let me inspect his bicep.

And that began an Official Office Survey.

The Official Office Survey was traditional in the days before Google came along and answered every question with the click of a button. Whenever an interesting topic of conversation raised a question that no one had a quick and certain answer to, an Official Office Survey was taken. Every patient who came through the door that day had the question put to them, and a consensus of opinion was eventually formed. The day ended with a phone call to the local library, where their helpful research staff happily pulled a volume off a dusty shelf and called us back in half and hour with the official answer.

On this occasion the question was a simple one. Do you think you could take Dr. Heath in a wrestling match? I asked everyone who came into the office that day and the next, and the feeling was universal. Yes, they all thought they could. If we had called the ladies at the library, I had the uneasy feeling that even they would have felt confident.

Finally, a young girl sat in my chair wearing a friendship ring that was wrapped with yarn to help it fit.

"Boy friend?" I asked, indicating the ring.

"Yes," she said.

"How old is he?" I asked.

"Fifteen," she said. "His name is Wesley."

"Do you think Wesley could take me in a wrestling match?" I asked, finally coming to my point.

She giggled and answered, "Of course," without hesitation, and that ended the survey. If I looked like I could be beaten up by a fifteen-year-old named Wesley, I didn't want to know about it.

Later that night, though, I stood in front of the mirror, and I studied myself critically from all angles. Finally, I turned sideways, and I slapped my belly. "Nah," I said, "I still got it."

Name That Tune

On a pleasant evening in October, when Corielle was seven and Tony was five, we went out for supper at Die Bier Stube, a German restaurant in downtown Frankfort. As we sat enjoying our bratwurst and sauerkraut, low music played in the background. You know the music I mean. A popular song from long ago, remixed to create a mellow, easy listening sound. You hear it, but only in the background. It's meant to simply create a mood.

Suddenly, Cindy cocked an ear, and a look of recognition came onto her face. "Fifty dollars to the person who came name that tune!" she said.

I listened carefully for a moment, and then, to the wonder and amazement of everyone, including our waiter, the cook, and strangers at nearby tables, I said, "*Chiquitita*, by Abba." It was the most miraculous occurrence imaginable. That I should recognize *any* song and be able to recall its name was unlikely, but that I was able to come up with the title of a seventies tune by an obscure Swedish band was unthinkable. Cindy sat with her mouth open, staring at me in amazement, but I was several steps ahead of her. I saw the opportunity to teach the kids a valuable life-lesson.

There is a theory that a child is a blank canvas, onto which we as parents can paint what we will. The idea is that as they grow, we apply small and delicate brush strokes, gradually and carefully crafting a completed picture. Until, on their twenty-first birthday, a whole and marvelous masterpiece of a human being stands before us. It's hogwash, of course, but the idea is mesmerizing, and we can't help but try. We blunder on, hoping our words will enter their empty heads, and some might become lodged and overlooked in a corner and perhaps take up residence permanently.

"Fifty dollars, please," I said, and I held out my hand.

"What?" Cindy asked, puzzled.

"Fifty dollars," I repeated. "You said, fifty dollars to the person who could name that tune, and I named it. Fifty dollars, please."

Cindy continued to look at me in confusion.

"You see," I said, turning to the kids. "Mommy bet Daddy that he wouldn't know something, but he did. Now Mommy has to pay Daddy fifty dollars!"

I went on, expounding on the dangers of gambling, the heartbreak of losing a bet, and the importance of being able to pay your losses promptly, as Cindy dug through her purse and came up with fifty dollars. She passed the money across the table, where I received it with great fanfare and folded it into my pocket.

After supper, we walked down the street to a little sweet shop on the second floor of the Trolley Barn mall, where we ordered ice-cream cones for dessert. As we left the store and headed back down the stairs, I heard the mall's sound system playing its own music, and miraculously, for the second time in a single night, I recognized the song. Seizing the opportunity to return Cindy's money, I turned and looked toward the top of the stairs. Cindy and Tony were just starting down. "Fifty dollars," I called out, "to anyone who can name *this* tune."

"What?" Cindy replied, not having heard me.

I amended my offer, because my largesse extended only so far. "Fifty dollars," I repeated more loudly, "to the person who can name this tune in the next three seconds... three... two..."

And Tony shouted, *"Don't Cry for Me Argentina!"*

"What?" Cindy said again, but it was too late. I was tangled in my own nets. I had just given a huge lecture about the evils of gambling and the importance of paying debts, and now I had lost a fifty-dollar bet to a five-year-old!

I handed Cindy's folded fifty dollars into the sticky hand of an overjoyed Tony and watched as he disappeared down the stairs and into the shops of the Trolley Barn. What else could I do?

Later, as we walked back to the car, Tony was carrying a brand-new stuffed cheetah, and Corielle was tugging at my sleeve and begging, "Somebody bet with me! Somebody make a bet with me!"

"I don't think the kids learned the lesson I was hoping they would," I grumbled.

"No," Cindy agreed, "I'm pretty sure they missed it. I'm not sure what you're complaining about though," she went on. "I'm the one that's out fifty dollars. "

That was true, I allowed, and I felt better after that. Maybe I should have taught the kids a lesson about playing with house money.

The Sneaky Beast

Skin cancer is a sneaky beast.

I see the dermatologist every six months for screening exams, and I've never once pointed out an area of concern that turned out to be anything at all. I've had two squamous cell carcinomas removed and one basal cell, but each time I'd pointed out a completely different thing to the doctor as my area of concern.

"Do you have any areas you'd like me to look at today?" Dr. Lipinski will ask.

"Yes," I will admit, "I have a bump on my shoulder that itches and tends to bleed when I scratch at it."

"Ok, no. This is nothing," the doctor will reassure me after a quick look, "but this thing over here needs to come off," and a spot will be pointed out that had escaped my attention altogether. So, since I apparently have no idea at all what I should be looking for, and my skin seems to be intent on killing me, I go to the dermatologist every six months, and I really don't think that's fair.

If you are tall, have a dark complexion, and happen to be handsome, there's a saying about you. If you have red hair and freckles, as I do, there's a saying about you as well, and it's this: Red hair - Mother Nature's warning label. And to add injury to insult, while Tall, Dark, and Handsome tans to a golden brown, my red-headed brethren and I spend our lifetimes burning and peeling. After a week in the Islands, Tall and Dark returns to work and hears, "Somebody's been on vacation. Look at that tan!" But not me. If I've been out of the office for a week, soaking up the sun on a beach somewhere, when I return to work people tend to assume I've been out sick.

And I didn't just rush off, willy-nilly, on vacation either. My skin, when left in its natural state, glowed a startling, fish-belly white that frightened children, so I prepared. I did tanning bed sessions for two weeks before any vacation in order to build a base and avoid a sunburn. My goal in the tanning salon didn't even rise to the level of getting a tan. I simply hoped to arrive at my destination and not be the whitest guy on the beach.

I felt self-conscious even in the tanning salon. I got bullied by young women with bronzed skin. Skin that forty years from now they might use to make baseball gloves. They were signing up for thirty minutes in a bed they called the George Foreman, and they looked at me with amusement and pity as I asked if the timer on my bed could be set to less than five minutes, because if I tanned for longer than that I had to take time off to recover. I imagine that those girls had the same tan all over, but I, myself, did not, because my tan was only apparent if you could see a tan line. I often tugged down the waist band of my swim trunks and exposed a crescent of lily-white cheek just to convince someone I had color.

Of course, I don't do tanning sessions anymore. Research indicates that the damage done to skin in tanning salons may have been worse than that done by the sun itself, so now, and for the rest of my life, I have to worry about skin cancer. Those with my complexion, I'm told, who have suffered one or more peeling sunburns, have a lifetime of increased risk for skin cancer.

For me, as a child, a peeling sunburn simply meant that summer had arrived. We had nothing like an SPF 30 sunscreen. Suntan lotions were more moisturizer than protectant. Their only benefit to me was that when my skin peeled away it was soft and pliable. I had many burns that caused my skin to peel in sheets large enough that, if done carefully, they could have been reassembled into a translucent and anatomically correct version of myself.

And so, I eventually decided to visit a dermatologist for a preventive screening as a hedge against the dangers of undetected skin cancer. I picked Dr. Lipinski, who had a listing in the Chamber of Commerce directory, and who sounded trustworthy. Like Dr. Kildare or Marcus Welby, who you may or may not have heard of, depending on how much television you watched in the sixties.

Upon my arrival, I was ushered into an examination room and left with a thin paper gown and instructions to put it on with the opening in the back. I stripped to my tighty-whities, slipped into the gown, and perched on the edge of the exam table on top of a slab of butcher paper. Soon, Dr. Lipinski walked into the room. At least I assumed it was Dr. Lipinski. She was, after all, wearing a white lab coat with a name tag that proclaimed as much, but she was very young and quite attractive, and she didn't look at all like Marcus Welby.

She smiled a radiant smile. "Good morning, Dr. Heath," she said. "I think we've met before. At a Chamber of Commerce golf outing maybe?"

Now perhaps you can engage in witty repartee while sitting on a slab of butcher paper in a thin paper gown, but I cannot.

"Maybe," I said hesitantly.

Her smile stayed determinedly in place. "You're here for the skin cancer screening. Is that right?"

I suddenly remembered that beneath my paper gown I wore tighty-whities that were neither tight nor white in the truest sense of the words.

"Um, yes?" I ventured.

She could see at this point that I was a man of few words, and her smile slipped. "Ok, then," she said briskly, "just hop down from the table and slip the gown off."

I stood in the center of the room with the gown in a puddle around my ankles. Following her instructions, I raised my arms from my sides and placed my feet apart while she lowered a pair of magnifying loupes and began to trace her fingers lightly over my skin as if she were reading me in braille.

The examination didn't take long, and after she'd frozen a few spots with an aerosol of liquid nitrogen I was sent home with a clean bill of health.

But I'm a redhead with a history of sunburns, and you can't be too careful. Ever since then I've gone back every six months, because skin cancer is a sneaky beast.

Last Words

I plan to live forever, but if that goal turns out to be unrealistic, that's all right too.

You see, dying is the inevitable price you pay for the privilege of having lived, and it's not even hard to do. Everybody does it. Even people who lived hundreds of years ago did it, and they didn't have the advantages offered by today's technology.

The trick, I think, is to do it well. Live your life like you're enjoying a fabulous meal, and when the check comes, throw your money down with a smile and leave a big tip.

Cindy's mom was the life of every party. She was funny, feisty, and full of life. As a younger woman, she was the one most likely to be found standing on top of the piano singing torch songs on New Year's Eve and waking up the next day in the bathtub. She loved to cook. She loved to laugh. She loved life. And I loved her like she was my own mother.

On a chilly March day in 1996, Cindy and I stopped by to visit her parents on a Sunday afternoon. We hadn't called ahead, because we knew they'd be home. They were always home.

Cindy was a child of her parent's later years. Her mom had been in her forties when Cindy was born, and now, well into her eighties, her health was in that rapid decline that you sometimes see in the very elderly. Over the past year she had become feeble and frail, and, although she was still bright and funny, with a quick wit and a sharp tongue, her mind had weakened along with her body.

She still read the *Tribune* every day, but now it was commonplace for her to look up from the sports page and announce, "Oh, good! The White Sox have gotten Ozzie Guillen to manage for them. I always liked Ozzie." Then she would look back at the paper, only to look up a moment later and repeat, "Oh, good! The White Sox have gotten Ozzie Guillen to manage for them. I always liked Ozzie."

So, Mom and Dad didn't go out as often as they used to, and Dad seldom left Mom home alone. Yet, when we rang the doorbell, no one answered. We rang a second time and waited. After a third ring, we were resigning ourselves to having wasted a trip when we heard Mom's voice call from upstairs.

"Coming! I'm coming! Hold your horses."

I looked at Cindy in alarm. Her folks lived in a split-level, and the stairs leading from the upper level were carpeted and steep. Mom seldom navigated those steps anymore without assistance.

"Mom? Is that you?" we called through the closed door.

"I'm coming!" she repeated, but those words were immediately followed by the thumping, bumping, clumping noises that a bowling ball or an elderly woman might make when tumbling down a short flight of stairs.

Silence.

"Mom?" Cindy shouted, "Are you all right?"

"Is that you, Cindy?" she answered. "Yes, I'm fine."

"Can you open the door?" I asked hopefully, as I put my eye against the letter slot and tried to peep inside.

"No, I can't seem to get up," she said, although she didn't seem in the least put out by that fact.

"Is Dad home?" we asked.

"No, I don't think he is. Let me check. Pep?" she called out. "Pep, are you here?"

No answer.

"Oh, that man! No, I don't think he's here."

For the next twenty minutes we tried to coax Mom into a position where she might open the door, and all the while we circled the house looking for a gap in a window, a loose screen, an unbolted back door. Anything.

As we frantically searched, Mom chatted through the letter slot as if we were sitting at the kitchen table.

"Cindy, it's so nice of you to drop by. I'll put on some coffee just as soon as I get up."

We finally used a neighbor's phone to call Peppy, Cindy's brother, and he arrived with a spare key at the same moment that her dad returned with a half gallon of milk, and the paramedics pulled up in an ambulance. We all crowded into the foyer at the same time, where we found Mom lying crumpled at the foot of the stairs, her leg twisted at an unnatural angle, and her head resting in a puddle of blood.

She looked up into a constellation of worried faces.

"Oh, my goodness!" she said happily, "Peppy's here too? How wonderful. If I had known you were all coming, I would have cooked something."

The head injury was minor, as it turned out, but her hip was broken, and that was serious. Cindy pointed out that since I had rung the doorbell, I was, in effect, responsible, but that was just finger pointing.

Mom weathered her surgery well, in spite of her age and tenuous health. Unfortunately, after just a few weeks, a mysterious fever developed, and the doctors, fearing an intestinal torsion, scheduled a second surgery.

When Mom awoke in the recovery room for the second time, Cindy told her that the doctors hadn't found the source of her fever, but they *had* repaired an old hernia while they were in there rummaging about.

Mom circled a finger in the air. "Whoop de doo!" she said with a weak smile. Those were her last words. She drifted into unconsciousness and passed away a short time later.

Peppy was in Detroit, and although he had started for home the moment it became clear that Mom's recovery wasn't going well, he was still en-route when she died. We expected him within the hour, and, in order that he might have a private moment to say his goodbyes before Mom was taken away, she was moved back into her room. There she was disconnected from her tubes and lines and was arranged peacefully in her bed, as if asleep.

It had been a long night for everyone, and, as the sun came up, Cindy's dad went outside for a cigarette. I followed along to keep him company, and Cindy pulled a chair close to the bed and sat vigil with her mother. She had been there only a short time when a young doctor swept into the room with Mom's unopened chart clasped beneath his arm.

He greeted Cindy in a business-like manner.

"Hello," he said briskly. "I'm Doctor Smith. I was Mrs. Corso's anesthesiologist during her procedure yesterday. I'm sorry to disturb you, but I need to take just a moment to check and see how she's doing this morning." He paused for an instant as he looked at Mom more closely. "My," he said, as he lifted her wrist and fumbled with his stethoscope, "she looks pale."

Cindy stared at him in disbelief.

"She's dead," she pointed out with remarkable composure.

The young doctor's eyes opened wide, and he stared from Cindy to her mother, who lay quietly, in mute affirmation of Cindy's statement. He dropped her wrist, which had almost certainly failed to yield a pulse, and, with his mouth opening and closing but no sound ushered forth, he backed slowly out of the room.

He was last seen running down the hall without having uttered another word.

I came back a short time later, and Cindy explained what had just happened.

"And you told him she was dead?" I asked in disbelief.

"Well, yes," Cindy said. "What was I supposed to say?"

"Well," I suggested, "when he said she looked pale, you should have said, Really? Do you think so? And then you should have just stepped back and let him work, because shit was about to hit the fan!"

Cindy looked at me in disgust and turned away, but I didn't mind, because I was used to that. And besides, I knew Mom would have thought it was funny, and that knowing, that last joke shared between us, has kept her alive in my heart to this very day.

Last words come in many flavors, and most, like "Rosebud" or "Father, why have you forsaken me?" are tinged with anger or regret.

For my money, when it's my turn, I hope my last words are "Whoop de doo."

*In the years before we had children, we tried to
placate Mom with gifts of stuffed animals.*

Mom, probably ordering me out of her kitchen.

A Romantic Man

As the last days of July ticked away in 1996, I could look at the calendar and see the date circled in red. The thirty-first. It was our twentieth wedding anniversary, and I was making plans that were so completely out of character that someone should have been taking my temperature and insisting that I go lie down.

You see, I'm not a romantic man. Let's just establish that fact up front. In fact, the list of things that I'm not is a long one. I'm not considerate, compassionate, kind, thoughtful, or a good listener. The list goes on and on, and I won't bore you with the whole thing, but Cindy has it all written down if you really want to see it.

I do my best, though. I try to enjoy walks on beaches, cozy fires on winter evenings, and sharing deserts, but, alas, even during the most romantic walks on the beach, I find myself wishing I were playing volleyball. And honestly, even when I do my best, it isn't very good. The small spontaneous gestures of romance are completely beyond me, so I focus my limited resources on the big-ticket items: birthdays, anniversaries, and Valentine's Day.

Cindy was born on the eighth day of February, and I dread the second week of that month like you dread a root canal. Cindy's birthday and Valentine's Day are like a baseball double-header, and Valentine's Day is the night game. My efforts on her birthday have laid waste to my bullpen and come Valentine's Day I'm completely useless.

Anniversaries are no better. They come and they go, mostly unnoticed, except for the card that I picked up at the Speedway on my way home from work and signed against the steering wheel of the car while sitting in the driveway. But one year, the year of our twentieth, I vowed to do better, and I surprised Cindy with a romantic getaway weekend as an anniversary gift.

The kids were little, so I arranged for a sitter to come to the house and stay while we were gone, and I had Cindy's secretary secretly clear her work calendar. I booked a Bed and Breakfast in South Haven, Michigan, and I packed for both of us.

This was where it got tricky. Women travel with a mysterious collection of bathroom products, all of which I assume are essential and none of which I can identify. I've seen these things many times, of course, spread in a colorful array across the top of a hotel room sink, and I remember one item that looked like a safety razor, and another that was probably a deodorant stick, but that's as far as I'm prepared to guess. And then there are the clothes. Which shoes are comfortable for walking? Which go with what outfit? And, most importantly, what in the closet fits right now? It would never do to pack clothes that are too tight. But perhaps it would be worse to pack those that are too loose.

For a moment I was frozen with indecision, until suddenly I was struck with inspiration. I packed only lingerie! Frilly, naughty, lacey things with no discernible function beyond decoration! You women may scoff, but trust me, your husbands are looking for a pen right now and writing this down on the palms of their hands. Not only did my plan solve the size problem and deal with the items of necessity issue, but it was sending a very clear message that could only be seen as romantic. And on our first day in South Haven, we would shop! Together we would browse shops and boutiques, picking out shoes, toiletries, and resort-casual outfits. I would be her metro-sexual, romantic hero.

The day arrived, and with a suitcase filled with teddies and chemises, I drove to Cindy's office and swept her away from her desk late on a Thursday afternoon. We stopped along the way for a late supper, and we arrived at the B&B after their front desk had closed for the night. I had anticipated this, however, and so we found a key under the mat, with a short note of welcome. It cautioned us to be as quiet as possible, as many of the other guests would already be asleep, and it directed us to our room on the third floor.

The room was a wonderland of fluffy bedcovers and lilac wallpaper. The bed was a four-poster that you needed a little stepstool to climb into, and over in the corner stood a large two person Jacuzzi. The room was oozing romance, and I immediately started water running into the tub. "While you're doing that," Cindy said, "I'm going to run down to the front desk and sign us in."

"Ok," I said, "but be quiet. Everybody else is asleep." She left, and I pushed the door gently shut behind her. I puttered around the room, unpacking, and when the tub was filled, I turned on the jets and eased myself in. I sank to my neck in hot water and bubbles. This romantic stuff, I thought, was not so hard. I even seemed to be developing a knack for it.

I continued to congratulate myself for several minutes more, and then I began to build little houses made of bubbles. After some time, I had constructed quite an elaborate city of soap bubbles. In fact, several distinct and separate soap-bubble civilizations had risen and fallen away to ruin when the water finally began to cool. I climbed out and toweled dry. Cindy's whereabouts had become a mystery of increasing aggravation with each passing minute. I mean, really, she knew I was upstairs, waiting, in a room with lilacs on the wallpaper, and fluffy bedspreads, and a tub of hot water with bubbles, and still she had been gone for nearly an hour.

I opened the door to the hall to start a search and nearly tripped over her recumbent form. She was lying propped against the wall next to the door, sound asleep. It appears that when I had pushed the door shut, it had locked behind her, and when she returned from the lobby moments later, after signing in, she found herself locked out. She knocked lightly to avoid waking the other guests, but over the noise of the running water and the Jacuzzi jets, I heard nothing. She continued to tap patiently, eventually sitting on the floor and knocking periodically at the lower corner, until she finally drifted off to sleep.

I contritely let her back into the room, where she climbed the step-stool into bed and dropped immediately back to sleep.

The next day found us on the streets of South Haven, moving at a leisurely pace from store to store, picking out vacation outfits for Cindy. It was a beautiful day in late July, and, as the sun glinted off the nearby waters of Lake Michigan, my hopes for a romantic weekend began to rebound. Granted, I had gotten off to a poor start by locking Cindy out of the room and forcing her to sleep in the hallway while I enjoyed a warm bath, but perhaps today was another day.

We stopped in the late morning for a sandwich at a lake-side café, and I ordered tuna fish while Cindy chose the chicken salad. After we finished, we gathered our bags together and started off hand in hand, walking back to the Bed and Breakfast. It was only a few blocks away, but as we neared the hotel, Cindy began tugging at my hand.

"Let's hurry," she said.

Yes! The clothes shopping idea was paying off already!

We hurried up the stairs to our room, and Cindy disappeared into the bathroom while I pulled off my shoes and climbed the step to sit on the edge of the bed. I was loosening my shirt when a series of explosive noises coming through the bathroom door made it clear that perhaps today wasn't another day after all.

"Are you ok?" I asked.

"I don't think the chicken salad was a good idea," Cindy gasped as sounds of retching and events more ominous resumed.

"Are you going to be in there for awhile?" I called through the door, because, you see, after all, I am a caring and compassionate man.

"I think so," Cindy admitted. "Why don't you go for a walk on the beach or something?"

So I did.

And about a quarter mile into my walk I joined a beach volleyball game, so, in a way, everything ended happily after all.

The Golden Age

There is a golden age for parents, which we need to recognize and appreciate. It's the age during which we're heroes to our children. We're surrounded, in their eyes, by a golden glow. They think we know everything, that we can do anything, and their greatest joy is to be with us. But, like a glorious sunrise, it's easy to miss, and it's soon gone.

Before we know it, we're being asked to drop our children off at the end of the block instead of in front of their friend's house, and they can't believe we wear *those* pants. But, during the Golden Age, life is wonderful, and we should savor it. Which is how I came to be singing *I'm in Love with a Big Blue Frog* while accompanied by a reluctant stranger on the piano.

It began earlier that same year. Corielle's birthday fell on a Wednesday, my day off, and she and I made plans for a special birthday treat. I was going to pick up pizza and bring it to her at school, where I would join her and her friends at lunch – as a *special treat*. The day would come, I knew, when that would be the worst punishment I could invent. But today, as she got on the bus, she climbed onto the first step, then turned. "See you at lunch today, Daddy!" she called.

"You bet!" I shouted back. "Happy Birthday! See you then!"

A little after noon, the phone rang, and I got up from whatever trivial task I was absorbed in and answered. A trembling voice was on the other end. "Daddy?" It was Corielle.

"What's wrong, Honey?" I asked.

"Daddy, are you coming to lunch?"

Lights exploded in my head. "Lunch? What? Yes! Shit! No. Sorry. What time is it?"

"Lunch is over Daddy."

I had completely forgotten. Forgotten so completely, in fact, that even hearing her voice hadn't rung any bells. It took her asking if I was coming to awaken me to the fact that I'd already missed it.

I hung up the phone and dashed to the grocery. I picked up a granola bar, a birthday card, a balloon, and a bouquet of flowers. When I walked through the front door of the school, my arms full of peace offerings, the receptionist looked up. "You must be Corielle's father," she said. "Down the hall, third door on your left."

Her scowl of disapproval followed me out the door. Apparently, the entire school was privy to my poor parenting.

I knocked on the third door down, and let myself in. Class was in session but came to a halt as I walked to Corielle's desk. In the eerie silence I crouched down next to her. "I'm so sorry, Honey," I said. "I just forgot. Here's a granola bar instead of pizza. I got you a balloon with a birthday card, and these are what boys call Jerk Flowers. We give them to girls we love when we know we've been a jerk. These probably won't be the last you ever get, but I hope they'll be the last ones you get from me."

I talked to her teacher later, and she said it wasn't uncommon for kids to forget to bring their lunch, but when that happened all the teachers donated a bit of theirs, so the child didn't go hungry. They'd offered that to Corielle, but Corielle had turned them down. "No," she kept saying. "My Daddy's going to bring pizza."

I had completely squandered a piece of the Golden Age. I had slept through the sunrise. Which brings us back to the big blue frog.

The Lincoln-Way Community Theater was going to perform *The Wizard of Oz*, and Tony was going to be in the chorus as a Munchkin. It would be awesome, he told me, if I were in the play with him. And after my recent fiasco with Corielle's birthday lunch, this was like a Golden Age do-over. I jumped at the chance.

It required that I audition for a part, and I picked up a flyer that said I should come prepared to perform a monologue and sing eight bars of the song of my choice. I called my friend Mike to find out what they meant by a monologue. Mike was an actual actor. He had an Actor's Equity card and had even been in commercials I'd seen on television.

"A monologue," Mike explained, "is usually a short piece from the play you're auditioning for, but it could be a favorite piece from another play, or even something you wrote yourself."

Now, I'm not a big fan of *The Wizard of Oz*, because the Flying Monkeys scare me, but I've always been fascinated by a glaring error made by the Scarecrow near the end of the movie. After he's handed a diploma by the wizard, he puts a finger to his head, and then he mangles the Pythagorean theorem. Gets it completely wrong. Butchers it. You don't make a gaffe of that magnitude without there being consequences, and that would be my monologue. What happened to the Scarecrow after Dorothy left Oz.

Several days later, I arrived for the audition with my music in one hand, and my monologue in the other. I was called into the audition room, where the director told me to give my music to the accompanist.

"What part will you be auditioning for?" he asked.

"The Scarecrow," I answered with completely unwarranted confidence.

"All right," he said, "we'll start with your song. What are you going to sing?"

I had hoped to lead with my monologue. The singing, I knew, was not going to be my strong suit. I had no ear for music. When I clapped along to a song, I clapped on one and three, which Cindy informed me was wrong. But I had no idea why, or even what the numbers meant. But I had picked a tune that I thought I could manage, and I handed over my music. "I'm going to sing *I'm in Love with a Big Blue Frog*, by Peter, Paul, and Mary," I said.

The director arched an eyebrow and looked at the pianist, who shrugged his shoulders and began.

I'm not sure how much eight bars are, but I'm pretty sure I only got through two of them before the director called out in a loud voice, "Thank you! Thank you. As much as I'd like to find out how this all turns out... I don't think I will."

And that was that. They showed me to the door. I never even got to read my monologue. But I did get a part in the play. I got the part of Uncle Henry who grumps around the farm at the very beginning of the play and again at the end. It isn't a singing part. All he has to do is look grumpy. Apparently, I nailed that in my audition as I stomped out the door with my unread monologue in my hand.

I wasn't really upset, though. This was the Golden Age, and Tony and I had an awesome time together doing the play. I just wish Corielle had been there. I'd have brought pizza.

When Sphincters Relax

I was helping Tony straighten his tie when a memory forced its way to the surface of my brain. A memory so powerful that from a distance of thirty-five years, it made my ears burn with embarrassment. I took Tony by the shoulders, turned him, and looked him in the eye. "Tony," I said, in my fatherly advice voice, "be sure to use the bathroom before you leave the house tonight."

Tony was getting ready for the Eighth Grade Social, which was an event along the lines of a miniature Prom, except the boys involved were awkward fourteen-year-olds dressed in black pants and white shirts, while the girls looked more mature than their years, wearing makeup and high heels.

Everyone remembers their first date. Some are awkward. Others are magical. Maybe you were an early bloomer, or went to an Eighth Grade Social, and you were only fourteen years old. Maybe you were confident and sophisticated, and you knew instinctively where to put your nose when you kissed.

I was none of those things. I was seventeen years old. I had grown up on a farm ten miles from the nearest town, and my social opportunities had been limited. Also, my hair stuck out from my head at odd angles, and my black-framed glasses were nearly always broken and taped together at the temple. And, since I'm being completely honest, I weighed less than one hundred pounds soaking wet and stood an even five feet tall with my shoes on.

I was a shy boy, if you can believe that, in spite of my physical gifts, and girls made my tongue stick to the roof of my mouth. Girls also had the unfortunate habit of giggling amongst themselves whenever I walked by, even though I had seldom said anything funny.

And yet, while some of us may not plunge into the water, we all eventually dip our toes into the dating pool, and I was no exception. The McPeek family farmed a place just down the road from us, and they had a daughter named Sylvia. She was younger than me, although a head taller, and she was pretty, in that robust, bursting out of their skin sort of a way that country girls have, and I made up my mind to ask her out on a date.

The asking, I knew, had to be done carefully, or it would end badly. First of all, so that the absurdity of my request didn't occur to her, it would be best if she wasn't given a great deal of time to think. I also didn't want her to be in a position to focus her attention too closely on me, or the hair and the glasses might become obvious. And finally, it would be better if she were sitting down, so that we were more nearly the same height.

Luckily we rode the same school bus, and I made a simple plan. I would wait until the bus was about to stop at my house, and then I would ambush her with the invitation. That way, no matter how things turned out, I had an exit strategy. This left no time for small talk, but small talk wasn't a part of my plan.

The next day, as the bus slowed to a stop at the top of our driveway, I dropped unexpectedly into the seat next to Sylvia. She looked up with alarm, as if geese had flown overhead, and I was the result. "Would you like to see a movie with me tomorrow night?" I blurted. I don't recall that I had ever spoken to her before that moment, but she, due to the genius of my plan, was taken completely off guard and reflexively said yes.

Now, let me digress for a moment in order to explain to you an odd thing about farmers. Although we live in the midst of nature at its most natural, surrounded by animals urinating, defecating, and procreating, we are very delicate in our own sensibilities, and the very mention of our bodily functions causes us extreme embarrassment.

At least, that was how it was for me. Which was why, getting back to my story, I should have used the bathroom before I left the house the next night. Instead, as I stood by my car a short while later, holding open the door as Sylvia climbed in, I realized that I had to pee. Now, I know it would seem to be a simple thing to ask to use her bathroom before we left, but the very thought made my ears go red and my tongue cling more tightly to the roof of my mouth, so I climbed into the driver's seat and we struck out for town.

The movie was in Freeport, a half hour's drive away, and by the time we arrived my situation was more urgent. The opportunity was there to use the washroom as soon as we bought our tickets, but I couldn't. Sylvia was standing right there. Beside me. Even if I left without saying anything, she would see where I'd gone, so we took our tickets and crossed the lobby to the concession area. I paid for popcorn and two large Cokes, and as we moved away from the counter, I looked longingly at the Men's Room sign, but we passed through the heavy purple curtains into the darkened theater and the opportunity was lost.

Throughout the Preview of Coming Attractions, I pondered my situation. Sylvia might have to go herself, I thought hopefully, and while she was away, I could slip out and see to my own business, but, unlike me, she must have gone before she left the house, and she remained in her seat. If she finished her drink, I reasoned, I could buy her another, and while in the lobby I could visit the washroom. I could use the same excuse, of course, to get a second popcorn, should we finish the first, so I began to shovel popcorn into my mouth. Which made me thirsty. Which led to the Coke. Which was a mistake.

Honestly though, no matter the excuse I used to leave my seat, I was afraid she would guess the truth, so I stayed where I was, and I crossed my legs.

When the movie ended, I hurried Sylvia toward the exit. My condition had become life threatening by this point. I had heard that it was possible to die from a burst bladder, and I had also heard that when people die, their sphincters relax. A horrible image of myself lying dead on the floor in a puddle of urine fixed itself in my mind's eye.

As we crossed the lobby, I looked again at the restroom, slowing down as we passed, giving Sylvia every opportunity to take the initiative, but she didn't so much as turn her head in that direction. Once outside, I hurried along the sidewalk and Sylvia ran to keep up. I held the car door impatiently, standing first on one foot and then the other, and pushed her inside. Any thoughts of stopping for a burger were abandoned. My only goal was to get her home before I died and my sphincters relaxed. The ride was twenty miles, and I hoped to do it in ten minutes. Halfway home, I knew I couldn't make it.

In desperation I pulled off the road, turned to Sylvia, and announced loudly, "I think we have a flat tire. I'll go check!" I jumped from the car before it stopped rolling and ran to the left rear tire. I dropped to my knees, and as I pretended to inspect the tire, I let loose the forces of evil from my body. Such blessed relief! You can't know if you've never been in that situation, but all was suddenly right with the world. Birds were singing! It was nearly midnight, but I swear to you, birds were singing.

And just then, when there was no turning back, no stemming the tide, no stopping the... well, you get the idea, the passenger door opened, and Sylvia got out to help with the tire.

I won't blame you if you don't believe me, but that's as much as I can remember of this particular date. I'm as certain as you are that there was more, and that it was horrible, but I have an amnesia that protects me.

And yet, thirty-five years later, I took Tony by the shoulders, and I looked into his eyes. "Make sure to use the bathroom before you leave the house tonight," I said.

Because, seriously, something like that would end up on YouTube today.

Just the Right Amount of Crastination

Valentine's Day was yesterday, and today I took down my Christmas lights.

Well, no, that's a lie. But I do hope to get to them maybe next week.

You see, I procrastinate. I don't know why, but sometimes I just can't seem to lever myself out of a chair. I know there are things to be done, and I know I should be doing them, but I just can't. I've always been this way, and I'm not alone. There are many out there who put off doing what ought to be done today, and maybe you're one of them, but, with more than a little pride, I claim to be in a class by myself.

You see, I'm not talking about little things, like waiting for that light to come on before filling your tank with gas, I'm talking about Olympic caliber procrastination. The sort of thing where afterwards you have to take a urine test to rule out Procrastination Enhancing Drugs. Years ago, I nearly failed to earn my dental license because I forgot to sign up for the licensing exam. Time slipped away from me. Four years of Dental School, and then one day all of my classmates were opening official looking letters confirming their registration for the upcoming Dental Board exams, and I was sitting in the Dean's office explaining that I had meant to sign up, I really had.

He had my permanent record lying unopened on the desk in front of him. "I'm sorry," he said, "I'm afraid there won't be much I can do." Then he opened my file and looked down at my transcript for a moment before looking back up. "It says here," he said slowly, "that you rank among the top ten students of your class. You've been elected to the OKU National Dental Honor Society, and you've already been accepted into a spot in a Dental Residency program... and you *forgot* to sign up for the Board Exams? Your entire class registered for this exam together. All on the same day!"

I lowered my eyes in pretended contrition, but my heart swelled as I realized again that I really *was* in a Class by Myself. I remember the Dean's face that day. He looked tired and confused. He sighed and said he would see what he could do, and then he waved me out of his office. If it had been possible, I'm sure he would have asked that I leave a urine sample with his secretary on my way out.

The Dean had to make a phone call to a Senator, it was later explained to me, and somehow my name magically appeared on the list of candidates for the Dental Board exams. It was a very near thing. But for the Dean's efforts and a Senator's intervention, I might very well be homeless today. It should be my lot in life to shake a cup on a sidewalk downtown while passer-bys look at me and then turn their heads away. "How sad," they whisper, "He was this close to becoming a dentist."

Luckily, I married Cindy, who, I would have to say, is the opposite of a procrastinator. She is an anti-crastinator, and between the two of us, we have just the right amount of crastination in our family.

Cindy makes lists, and I see them lying on the top of her dresser. The lists have headings like, "Things to do tomorrow," and there will follow as many as ten items, some with tic marks beside them, indicating, I suppose, that they have already been completed. And it isn't even tomorrow yet! If I had a list headed, "Things to do tomorrow", it would be on a soiled scrap of paper stuck to a lemonhead and a piece of lint in my jeans pocket, and it would read simply, "Call Ken about golf", and there wouldn't be a tic mark by it because I probably never got around to it.

Cindy is retired, and by that, I mean she doesn't have a job that pays her money anymore. Do you know what I would do if I were retired? Well, I don't either, but it would involve sleeping in, I can tell you that much. And yet every morning Cindy gets up before I do, and she bustles about the house, looking at a list held in her hand and mumbling, "I have so much to do today. I have a Village meeting at 8:30, then breakfast with the girls, then pick up Tony's trombone, exercise at Curves, back here to let in the repair guy," and she disappears out the backdoor, leaving an impossible cloud of tasks floating in the air behind her like that little puff of dust a cartoon character leaves when he darts off.

And I, meanwhile, am sitting at the breakfast table, with my mouth full of half chewed Cheerios, wondering if I'll have time to brush my teeth before I go to the office, or if maybe I shouldn't just leave that for in the evening.

I honestly don't believe I've ever had a day filled with as many things to do as Cindy manages on an every-day basis. Just listening to her tell me how busy she's going to be wears me out. And yet, when I do get one of my occasional chores completed, I'm filled with an inordinate pride. Cindy may tic ten items off her list on a daily basis, but one day soon I'm going to take down the Christmas lights, and on that day, I'm going to sit down in my chair, lean back, and reflect on a job well done.

And Cindy will hurry past mumbling, "At ten I have a meeting with the Mayor, then Play practice at the Middle school, then rehearse with the Solo and Ensemble kids,..."

I Love Halloween

In my house, I have a cedar chest filled with costume items, and at a moment's notice I can turn myself out as a witch, a pirate, a prison inmate, a Keystone Cop, or a sexy nurse. I even have my own makeup, including foundation, rouge, eye liner, and a nice pink lipstick, because Cindy hates it when I use hers. I will entertain any excuse when it comes to getting dressed up in costume, but Halloween is a special treat. I love Halloween.

I have a patient who is a professional makeup artist, and he comes to my house before six on Halloween morning and turns me into the character of my choice. Over the years, he's done me as a werewolf, a scarecrow, Puss n' Boots, The Cat in the Hat, Uncle Fester, Beetle Juice, and Captain Jack Sparrow. The makeup takes over an hour to apply, and when he's finished, I don't even recognize myself.

Having gone to this effort, of course, I wear my costume all day. I wear it to the office, working on patients, and when it's time for Trick or Treat, I answer the door in costume. And if, in my opinion, the costume of the child ringing my doorbell is lacking in sincerity or conviction, if they're just going through the motions without putting in any real effort, I will reach into their bag, remove a piece of candy, and close the door in their startled little faces.

Now, before you get your undies in a bunch, let me say that I don't do this to the little kids. The little kids are cute. They're dressed up like Spiderman or Barack Obama, and I happily give them candy. I'm talking about the big kids. The High School Kids. The ones whose costume consists of a hooded sweatshirt and some brown stuff rubbed onto their faces who claim to be a hobo. They sneer at you as they reach their gigantic hands into your candy bowl and shovel miniature Snickers bars into their bulging pillowcases. Those are the kids I mean. They disrespect the spirit of the Holiday, and I can't abide that. So, one year, I set out to stop them.

I made up a scarecrow and set him into a lawn chair at the end of the sidewalk nearest the driveway. He was dressed in a red flannel shirt, blue jeans, Handy-Andy work gloves, and tennis shoes. His head was a burlap sack stuffed with straw, and I posed him in the most realistic posture I could manage, so that to the casual eye he could be mistaken for human.

Then I dressed myself in an identical costume, right down to the burlap sack over my head. I stuffed straw up every cuff and down every collar, and I draped myself onto a chair set near the steps to the front door. I arranged my limbs into the most unnatural pose I could manage, so that I appeared more scarecrow-like than the one stuffed with straw. I set the bowl of candy on my lap and awaited the arrival of Trick or Treaters.

As the little ones came to the door, their parents in tow, I moved slowly and deliberately so that they could tell, well in advance, that I was alive. I silently held out the bowl of candy, and they, cautiously, at the urging of their parents ("Ha ha! Go ahead. He's a funny scarecrow!") dipped in a hand and retreated with their candy. I didn't want to scare the young ones. I was after larger prey.

As the evening wore on, the Trick or Treaters came less frequently, until finally, for long periods, I sat alone and quiet. The sun had slowly set until now it was fully dark. My pulse quickened. This was the hour of the High School Kids. Soon I heard them coming, their clamorous approach heard long before they could be seen. They trouped down the middle of the street in a large pack. The High

School Kids always travel in large packs. They came to the cul-de-sac and finally onto my driveway.

I slumped in my lawn chair and sat perfectly still, my breath slow and shallow so as not to move my chest. I listened as they discovered the first scarecrow. "Whoa!" they said, stopping some distance from the scarecrow. "What's that?" They moved closer as a group.

"It's a scarecrow," one said.

"OOhhh," said another, "I'm so scared!"

"It looks real," said a third.

One approached and cautiously poked it with his finger. "Nope," he said. "It's fake. Come on." And they passed by and continued up the sidewalk. I watched them through the gauzy filter afforded by my burlap mask. I could see at once, despite their hoodies and brown-smudged faces, that they were not real hobos. They rounded the bend in the sidewalk and saw me for the first time. "There's another one," they said and continued without a second look. When on the hunt, patience is a virtue, and I bided my time. To go too soon would diminish the effect.

Only when they were fully abreast of my position did I make my move. I exploded out of my seat with a hideous groan and thrust the bowl of candy into their very midst with both hands. The group levitated into the air, leaving puddles of urine on the sidewalk where each had stood. Like cartoon characters, they rose straight up, their legs spinning in a circular blur, and then with a puff, they rocketed off in all directions at once. Unfortunately for them, all directions were prickly. There was a hedge to their right, a magnolia behind, and Burning Bushes to their left, so that after only a brief flurry of frantic flight, they were all impaled in various positions inside the shrubbery.

Their panic was short-lived of course, and they were soon climbing down from and out of the magnolia and the hedge and the Burning Bushes, and cautiously taking pieces of candy from the bowl which I continued to hold out, now immobile and silent.

"Jesus, you scared me!" one said.

I didn't respond.

"You really look real, dude!" attempted another.

I remained immobile and silent.

"You are real, right?" ventured a third.

"Awesome costume!" they finally said, and they walked away with many nervous looks back over their shoulders.

I heard them talking amongst themselves as they moved away up the street.

"You were really scared!"

"No I wasn't!"

"You were so. You should have seen yourself jump!"

"No I never!"

And their voices faded into the distance as I settled back into my chair, rearranged my straw collar to its best advantage, and began the wait for the next group.

I love Halloween.

When you put this much effort into a costume,
you don't give candy to Hobos.

An In and Out Procedure

I am no longer a young man. I've gotten older, although I'm not sure when it happened. One day I was fine, and the next day I saw a picture of myself taken from above, and there was a large fleshy spot on the top of my head that I'm sure wasn't there before, and I had to go lie down and take a nap.

I play bridge in a group composed of similarly old men. We meet on the third Thursday of every month, and when we get together, being old, we talk about our ailments. We brag, actually, like it's a competition. If one of us complains of an enlarged prostate, the next has one the size of a baseball, and there's someone in the room who hasn't gone to the bathroom standing up in two years.

But, as fascinated as we all are by our prostate, our favorite subject is our bowel. We're all over fifty after all, and, if you're over fifty they say, it's time you had the doctor up onto the back porch for a visit, if you catch my drift. In case you didn't catch my drift, let me be clear. We are greatly amused by, and we talk at great length about, colonoscopies.

I put off having my first colonoscopy for as long as I dared. I knew the day would come eventually, but who wants to rush into a thing like that? I mean, you know what they do to you when they do a colonoscopy, right? If you don't, go right now and look it up on YouTube. I'll wait here while you do.

But shortly after my fiftieth birthday, I had two friends who were about my own age, and who passed away within a short time of one another, both from colon cancer, and I made an appointment with a doctor. Of course, I first had to find a doctor because I certainly didn't have one. Men don't "have" doctors. Women have doctors, and they see them annually. The doctors do horrible things to them, and yet they go religiously. And children have doctors because their mothers take them. But men? Our mothers are too old to take us anymore, and doctors are always putting a gloved finger where it doesn't belong, so we avoid them.

I eventually found a doctor, a general practitioner, and she was a very pleasant woman. She made an appointment for me to see a gastroenterologist, who would do the actual colonoscopy, and she explained the Prep procedure. For forty-eight hours, she said, I was to be on clear liquids. That's two full days of nothing but jello and beef bouillon, for those of you keeping a scorecard. Then, nine hours before the procedure, I was to mix a packet of powder with a glass of water and drink it down. Six hours later, I was to drink a second glass. I was to be driven to the med-center at six in the morning, and I would be home by ten. In her words, it was a simple "in and out" procedure. I looked at her closely to see if she were making a joke, but as far as I could tell she didn't find the same humor in colonoscopies that my bridge group did.

I was scheduled for the procedure on a Wednesday morning, but I work late on Tuesdays, so when the time came to drink the first glass of powder, I was still at the office. I wanted to stay on schedule, and I imagined that the powders needed time to work, so I considered drinking it between patients, but at the last moment I decided to wait until I got home. Now, this is important. Go get a pencil and write this down. If ever you should find yourself in this situation, *Do Not* drink the powders if you are not within sight of a bathroom! In fact, to be safe, drink the stuff while you are *in* the bathroom and already sitting down. And bring a book. You're going to be there for a long time.

It's like a science experiment! You all remember that science experiment you did when you were in the third grade, where you put vinegar into baking soda and made a volcano? It's like that volcano. So much should not be able to come out of an opening that small without leaving an exit wound. When it came time to drink the second glass of powders, my first volcano was still in the bathroom erupting! If I drank the second glass, there was no way I was going to be able to get into my car and drive to the med center in another two hours. I would happily have gotten into your car, but I was not getting into mine. So, I didn't drink it.

A couple of hours later, I lay in the pre-opp area at the med-center while Nurse Ratched took my history. "And did we take all of our medication as instructed by the doctor?" she asked.

"No, we did not." I admitted. "We didn't drink the second glass."

She looked at me sternly. "You know," she scolded, "if Doctor finds any 'material' up there, he may not be able to do the procedure."

"If Doctor finds anything at all up there," I said, looking her right in the eye, "I'll gladly eat it."

Add Nurse Ratched to the list of those who don't find colonoscopies funny.

She took me into the surgical room and laid me onto my side, with my surgical gown draped open so that my bare buttocks stuck out into the room like a lighthouse on a foggy shore. About six nurses were scurrying around the room and I was pretending to be invisible when the doctor walked in. He had my chart in his hand.

"So... Alan Heath?" he asked. I waved a hand over my shoulder to identify myself, just in case there happened to be more than one of us lying in the room with our buttocks in the air. "It says here you're a dentist," he said.

Oh, please God, no, I thought. He wants to chat!

I didn't answer. I lay there quietly, still pretending to be invisible and hoping he would go away, but he went on, "Are you Tony Heath's dad?" I slowly looked over my shoulder, as the realization seeped in. I was about to have a conversation with this man. With him speaking into my ass hole as if it were a microphone.

"How do you know Tony?" I asked politely.

It turned out that his son and my son were friends at school. We talked for what seemed like several hours, and all the while he held something in his hand that looked like a garden hose. He gestured with it gently as he spoke, and I watched it like a mongoose watches a snake. "Well," he said finally, "we might as well get started. If you want, you can watch the procedure on that TV monitor in front of you."

I turned back, and I saw that the garden hose apparently had a tiny camera mounted into the end of it, and on the TV screen I saw the doctor's face, then ceiling tiles, then a nurse, and then a sight that no man should ever see, and I closed my eyes.

And after that? Honestly? It wasn't so bad. It was a simple in and out procedure.

The Brotherhood of Men

It was ten o'clock on a Sunday morning, and I was in my office doing an emergency root canal when the phone rang. My assistant left her place beside the chair, and when she returned she addressed herself to the patient.

"Dell is in the hospital," she said, "and he's going to need surgery."

Twenty-four hours earlier, my assistant Tami, whose wedding day was fast approaching, had confessed that she was unhappy about her fiancée's upcoming bachelor party. "There are going to be strippers there," she complained. "Lesbian strippers! Why do men have to do stuff like that?"

I looked at her with surprise. I thought I had misunderstood the question, but I quickly changed my expression to one of fatherly concern. "Tami," I explained, "It's just guys being guys. Glenn loves you. Stop worrying." But she continued to fret throughout the day.

As we left the office that evening, she turned to me again. "I just have a bad feeling about tonight," she insisted.

"Tami, stop it," I said. "It's just a bachelor party. Everything's going to be fine."

Early the next morning the ringing of my bedside phone jarred me awake. "Dr. Heath?" It was Tami, her voice trembling with emotion. "The bachelor party didn't go so well," she continued. "Glenn got into a fight, and his lip is all cut up and swollen. He has two broken teeth, and I think he's going to need stitches and a root canal."

We met at the office a short time later, and as we worked, Tami told the story.

A bachelor party is the responsibility of the Best Man. It's one of very few responsibilities, really. They're spelled out in the Bride's magazine that every bride subscribes to. Duties of the Best Man: Show up in a tuxedo. Have a wedding ring in your pocket. Organize the bachelor party. That's it. It's not a lot to ask, and Glenn's bachelor party had been organized by his Best Man, Dell.

Dell arranged for the entertainment—the strippers—and picked a local bar as the venue. The guest list consisted of a small group of drinking buddies and Tami's older brother Bill. Which was unfortunate, because Bill and Glenn had never gotten along. Many brothers over the years have objected to their sister's choice of a husband, but Bill went at it like he was being paid by the piece.

Inside the bar, the group began an assault on several bottles of tequila. A tall glass was fetched from the kitchen for Glenn's use, and toast after toast was raised to the future groom, with Bill's contributions focusing mostly on Glenn's shortcomings and possible inability to fulfill his marital obligations. As Glenn tossed back the drinks, his tolerance for Bill decreased in proportion to the level of the bottle, and it was at this brittle juncture in the evening that Dell snapped his cell phone shut and announced that the strippers weren't going to be able to make it.

Groans of disappointment arose from all sides, and, as Glenn drained yet another glass of tequila, he turned his blurring gaze toward his future brother-in-law and came to a momentous decision. Bill was going to have to die. In fact, Bill's death was so clearly called for in Glenn's mind, that he was surprised he hadn't thought of it sooner. He realized that he had been putting off killing Bill for years now, and tonight, on the eve of his wedding and in the company of his friends and Jose Cuervo, the time had come.

Glenn began an unsteady pursuit of Bill, chasing him through the bar and out into the parking lot. The two were followed by the remainder of the party in a happy and boisterous knot, all of them grateful that if there weren't going to be strippers, at least there was going to be a fight. But, as it became clear that Glenn's intention was murder, Dell intervened by tackling him from behind and dragging him to the ground. Dell's concern wasn't for Bill, you understand, he simply felt that it was among his duties as Best Man to keep Glenn out of jail until after the wedding.

Glenn was a big man, much bigger than Dell, and it was only because Glenn was nearly too drunk to stand unassisted that Dell was able to hold him down at all. But as he sat astride Glenn's heaving chest, it was clear that it was only a matter of time before Glenn broke free and got on with the business of killing Bill.

"Dude," Dell begged, "settle down. If I can't hold you down, I'm gonna have to knock you out!"

Glenn was beyond caring, really, but, as a friend, he was willing to let Dell do whatever he felt was necessary. "Ok," he answered, as he continued to struggle, "I guess you'll have to go ahead with that then." Dell knew from watching movies that a simple rap on the jaw rendered people unconscious, so he doubled his fist and delivered a sharp blow, hitting Glenn flush in the mouth.

Glenn turned his head to the side and spit out a mouthful of bloody tooth fragments. "That didn't do it," he said through split lips. "You'll have to hit me again." Dell obliged by putting his full weight behind a second blow, this time lacerating his hand on a broken tooth and mercifully rendering Glenn unconscious.

Bill, who had earlier fled the scene, now returned, driving a pickup truck with the intention of running Glenn over as he lay in the middle of the parking lot in a puddle of blood, tequila, and broken teeth.

Luckily, the remainder of the group commandeered the vehicle and plucked a protesting Bill from behind the wheel before gathering Glenn by his wrists and ankles and flinging him, like a sack of turnips, into the bed of the pickup truck where he fell in a crumpled heap.

The lot of them then happily squeezed into the cab of the truck and drove to Tami's house, where they delivered her fiancé and left him propped in a corner of the shower, where he alternately bled into the drain and threw up for the rest of the night. Tami waited until seven o'clock the next morning before calling me at home.

"Dr. Heath?" she said, "The Bachelor Party didn't go so well."

Now, as we sat on either side of the dental chair with Glenn between us, still so drunk that Novocain was a formality, Tami finished her story. "Well," I said, "after all this, I suppose you need a new Best Man?" Just then the phone rang, and when Tami came back, she spoke to Glenn.

"Dell is in the hospital," she said. "He's going to need surgery. Apparently, he severed a tendon in the back of his hand. He'll have to wear a cast for a couple months."

Glenn half raised from the chair in alarm. "But we were supposed to go fishing next week," he said. "How can he throw out his line if he's wearing a cast?"

The next day, at the wedding, I watched Dell standing beside Glenn and Tami at the front of the church. His wrist was in a cast and his arm in a sling. He leaned on an IV pole dripping antibiotics through a long tube, and I felt proud to be a part of the brotherhood of men.

The General wore a Yellow Shirt

It was four in the morning, and I should have been in bed, but instead I was standing in the middle of Kansas Street, dressed up like General Patton, if General Patton had worn a yellow shirt, and a stranger was looking at me expectantly. It was Labor Day Weekend in Frankfort, and, like I said, I was wearing a yellow shirt.

Labor Day weekend in Frankfort has been taken over by the Frankfort Fall Festival since the 1950s, and I've been working it as a member of its organizational committee since moving here in the early '80s. I haven't been to a Labor Day picnic or pool party in forty years.

The volunteer committee members are identified by the yellow shirts they wear, and in fact, they refer to themselves by two names. Yellow Shirts, because of what they wear, and Street Walkers, because of what they do. (They walk the streets to keep the Festival running smoothly. Let's all keep our minds out of the gutter, shall we?) The yellow shirt is both a uniform and a badge of honor. It's worn proudly, and those who put it on shoulder responsibilities and gain authority by virtue of wearing it.

The Festival begins on a Saturday morning, and the two-hundred and fifty Crafters who line the streets with their booths begin setting up in the pre-dawn darkness. Every Craft booth is assigned a ten-by-ten-foot space at a specific location on a specific street, and the Yellow Shirts are asked to be on the streets before the sun comes up, to make sure they get there.

During the years that I served as Chairman of the Festival, it became tradition that we create a skit, or some sort of motivational entertainment to energize the volunteers before they took to the streets on that first morning. On this particular year, I had decided to give the speech made famous by George C. Scott at the opening of the movie *Patton*. That movie begins with General Patton standing in front of a huge American flag addressing the Third Army as they prepare for a great battle. "No poor bastard ever won a war by dying for his country!" he growls. "He won it by making the other poor bastard die for *his* country." It's a great speech, and, as my army of volunteers prepared to take to the streets that morning, I imagined it getting us off to a rousing start.

Of course, I couldn't give Patton's speech without dressing up in costume, so I had a General's Stars sewn onto the collar of my Yellow Shirt. My chest was festooned with every ribbon and medal I could find. I wore a shiny, silver WWII helmet, and I had a pair of pearl-handled revolvers strapped to my waist. I had an enormous fake butt with a huge plumber's crack rising from the back of my trousers for no better reason than that I owned an enormous fake butt, and I used it at every opportunity. Finally, I wore a rubber Halloween mask depicting the ruddy, unshaven face of a grumpy old man chomping on the stub of a cigar.

I parked my car at the far end of the Festival, behind the Trolley Barn, and, in the dark and chill of the pre-dawn morning, I began my march through the dimly lit streets toward the Volunteers' office. I was halfway down Kansas Street when a Crafter spotted my yellow shirt and grabbed me by the elbow. He thrust his face to within inches of mine. "This guy," he expostulated, pointing to his neighbor, "is setting his booth up almost a foot over into my space! I keep telling him he's too far over, but he just keeps setting up!! You have to tell him to move."

The Crafter stood, with his hands on his hips, and looked at me expectantly. I peered at him out of the tiny eye-holes of my rubber mask. The streetlight glinted off the pearl handles of my revolvers, and my plumber's crack glowed like the risen moon. I pushed the helmet higher onto my forehead and scratched my rubber chin thoughtfully. No flicker of concern darkened the face of the Crafter. No moment of dawning comprehension, no widening of the eyes. Nothing. All he saw was the yellow shirt.

"Well?" he said, tapping his foot in impatience. I turned to the second Crafter, who was standing nearby. He too looked at me without a trace of wonder.

"All right, Soldier," I began, my voice like tires on gravel, "I want you to break down this tent and move it back inside your designated coordinates." I paused and settled my revolvers more comfortably around my hips. "Then I want you to police the area," I continued, "and be set up and ready to sell by no later than 0900 hours! Is that clear, Soldier?"

"Yes, sir," he replied sheepishly, and immediately began to strike his tent.

"Good!" I said. "Carry on!" I took two steps away and then turned back. "Men?" I barked, "Make me proud today!" But they didn't hear me. They had both returned to their interrupted tasks without a second glance in my direction.

Which was too bad, really, because the sight of me marching off down Kansas street with my Plumber's crack glowing under the streetlights was truly motivational.

I am *Embarazado*

We took our first Cancun trip when the kids were young, and, after we cleared customs, we picked up our luggage and walked into Mexico through a set of double doors. We had reservations at a hotel in the heart of the tourist district, and I had our transportation voucher in my hand as we pushed our way through a crowded lobby on our way to the taxi stand.

We were surrounded by young men wearing crisply pressed uniforms of various descriptions as we made our way toward the outer doors. They circled, if we had bothered to notice, like sharks around a life raft.

One of the young men approached us. His name tag announced him to be Paul. "Senor! Amigo!" Paul called. "Do you have your transportation arranged?"

"Yes," I said, holding up my voucher, "we're all set."

"Ah, excellent!" he said, and he reached out and plucked it from my hand. "Allow me to assist you with your bags." Two other, equally polite young men swooped in and lifted our suitcases from our hands. "If you will follow me, please?" It had all happened so quickly. At no time did I suspect anything untoward was afoot, but suddenly I found myself with no luggage, and my transportation voucher was hurrying away toward a desk at the side of the room. We followed along quickly, protesting mildly. We didn't want to make a scene, because, after all, there was a chance that this was simply how things were done in Mexico. Perhaps there was a desk at which one had to sit as one's voucher was processed and one's luggage was taken to the appropriate location.

We were guided into chairs facing a desk at which Paul now sat. "How long will you be enjoying your stay with us in Cancun?" he asked.

"We'll be here for a week," I answered.

"Ah, excellent, excellent!" Paul responded, with every evidence of being truly delighted at the prospect of our visit. "Do you have any plans for activities or trips while you are here? Perhaps snorkel, or scuba? Maybe a visit to our famous ruins at Chichen Itza?"

He seemed to be an exceptionally curious young man. These were strange questions coming from a person whose job it was to assist us with our transportation to the hotel, but, yes, we admitted, we did have plans to do such things.

"Wonderful," Paul effused, but then a look of concern clouded his face. "But a trip to Chichen Itza normally costs one-hundred and fifty dollars, US," he said. And then his look brightened. "Perhaps, if you will allow me, I can arrange it for you for half of that!" and he looked so very happy at the prospect of providing us with this service. It turned out that all we had to do was take one hour of our time and visit the Royal Sands resort as his guest. He would even provide us with a complementary breakfast buffet on the morning of our tour.

What was one hour to us? We were on vacation. And that one hour came with a free breakfast and saved us seventy-five dollars on a trip we planned to take anyway! We signed up with enthusiasm. And after we had our luggage and voucher returned to us by Paul, and we began moving once again toward the outer doors, we were hijacked by a second young man, taken to a second desk, and signed up for another free breakfast and a second one-hour tour after this time being offered a free snorkel adventure.

In any event, we ended the week as the new owners of a time-share week at the Royal Sands resort, and, although we may have felt ambushed by the process, we never regretted the purchase. Over the next twenty years of nearly annual visits, it became a second home. We became familiar with the people, the place, and, to some extent, the language. As you may or may not be aware, they speak a completely different language in Mexico. Many feel that it's the world's responsibility to speak English, but I make every effort to attempt the native language when in a foreign country. However feeble those efforts might be.

My problem arises not in speaking, but in hearing. I hear more slowly than Mexicans speak. Given enough time, I can put together a question and deliver it with reasonable fluency. Sadly, this gives the person to whom I've directed my question the unfortunate impression that I speak the language. And their answer, delivered at Mexican speed, is completely incomprehensible to me. I don't even hear words. All I hear is "Blah Blah Blah," only with no pauses and no capital letters. Just, "blahblahblah." To which, rather than risk looking stupid, I reply, "Gracias" and wander off in a random direction trying to look purposeful.

At the Royal Resorts, they host a pool-side party on the Sunday of each week, and at that party, games are played, raffles are held, and free rums and cokes are drunk. If your name is drawn in a raffle, you might win dinner for two at a nice restaurant, or maybe a hat. My name was drawn the last time we were there, and as our host handed me a hat, he held a microphone to my face and asked where I was from.

"Chicago," I answered, and then, because I had taken advantage of the free rums and cokes, I added, "Go Bears! We play the Packers tomorrow on Monday Night Football."

"*Es verdad?*" he asked politely. "Who do you think will win?"

And since he had spoken a bit of Spanish to me, I decided to make a cautious effort of my own. "In Chicago," I said, "we don't really expect to win. We just hope that at the end of the game we're not *embarazado*."

See what I did there? I substituted the Spanish word *embarazado* for the English word embarrassed, thus giving the impression that I spoke Spanish without the dangers of trying to put together an entire sentence. This carried a reduced risk of looking stupid. I thought my quip was rather clever, and I was rewarded with a burst of laughter from the Spanish speakers in the audience. I returned to my lounge chair by the pool with a self-satisfied smile.

"You know," Cindy said as I sat down, "that *embarazado* does not mean embarrassed."

"It doesn't?" I asked.

"No," she said. "It means pregnant."

Well now, that's not really my fault, is it? It *should* mean embarrassed, or why else make it sound so much like it? But regardless of that, I thought, my remark was technically correct.

So, I got up from my chair, tried to look purposeful, and wandered off in a random direction.

Poolside at the Royal Sands, Trying to look purposeful.

That's Alphonso Bedoya

A young patient was reclined in my dental chair. His mouth was propped open and several teeth were isolated by a rubber dam. Tubing snaked from beneath the dam and a suction tip slurped noisily. I was inside his mouth with ten fingers and a high-speed handpiece.

Suddenly, something buzzed, and it startled me. I looked around wildly for just a second until my patient fumbled blindly into his pocket and came out with a cell phone. He lifted it to where he could see it from the corner of his eye and read its text message. He then dropped his hands into his lap and, with a flurry of thumbs, typed in a response.

The first time it happened I was startled and confused, but that was years ago. It happens all the time now, and although it doesn't bother me anymore, I admit I have no idea what they can possibly be talking about. Imagine yourself in the dental chair—your lip is numb, the drill is whining, and your tooth smells like burning hair—wouldn't you be fully present? Wouldn't you be focused on the here and now?

Of course, *you* would. But not the youth of America. They're never disconnected, and, as far as I can tell, they're never focused on the here and now. If I leave them alone in the chair for over a minute, when I return, they have their phone out. They're connected by an electronic tether. They might be talking, texting, surfing, or gaming, but they're doing something. And it's not just that they're doing something, it's that they're doing *something else*. It's the same when they watch a movie. They're not just watching the movie, they have their phones in their hands, and they're also doing something else.

When I was a kid, if some exciting event took place, days later I might tell my friends the story of what happened, probably making it better in the telling, and they never interrupted by saying, "Yeh, you posted that on Facebook."

If I sat down to dinner and was served an amazing desert, I never sent a picture of it to a friend. Granted, that would have been more difficult back then. I would have had to borrow my parents' camera, make sure I had a flash bulb, take the picture, wait months or possibly a year while they shot up the rest of the roll, get it to the drug store, wait a week until the photos were developed, pick them up, find an envelope, find a stamp, and mail the picture. But still, I could have done that, and I chose not to.

Arguments have been changed forever by Google. It used to be that a disagreement had substance and took up measurable time. A difference of opinion was an entertaining way to spend an evening. But not since Google. Now there's black and white. Right and wrong. There's no time and little tolerance for disagreement.

Let's take a look at a scene from long ago, which might have gone something like this:

(Scene: early evening. You're expecting friends for dinner. The doorbell rings. You answer by cracking the door and peeping out. Your friends are standing on the stoop.)

You: Let me see your badges.

They: Badges? We don't have no badges. We don't got to show you no stinking badges!

You: *(opening the door)* Ha ha! *Blazing Saddles.* I love that movie.

They: *Blazing Saddles?* No, that's from a John Wayne movie. Some guys were pretending to be the Federales.

You: It's from *Blazing Saddles*. The bad guys said it to Hedley Lamar, remember?

(End Scene)

That disagreement is going start a conversation that will fill the evening. You'll debate. You'll recall. You'll reminisce. You most likely won't agree on where the line about badges came from, but that was never really the point, was it?

Now, let's look at that scene as it occurs today.

(Scene: as before except now a cell phone chirps. It's a text message announcing that the guests have arrived and are standing on the stoop. Youth cracks open the door and peeps out.)

Youth: Let me see your badges.

They: Badges? We don't have no badges. We don't got to show you no stinking badges!

Youth: *(opening the door)* Ha ha! Ok, wait. Let me Google that. That's Alphonso Bedoya from *Treasure on the Sierra Madre*, 1948, starring Humphrey Bogart and directed by John Huston. It was Huston's third film. It featured a mismatched trio of adventurers, who are confronted by bandits who say, "Badges? We ain't got no badges. We don't need no badges! I don't have to show you any stinking badges!"

They: Ok… Hey, when do we eat? I hope it's not for awhile, because I was at the dentist earlier and my lip's still numb.

Youth: Yeh, you texted me from the chair, remember? And I read your blog and saw the pictures on Facebook. Plus, you tweeted when he hit the nerve.

A Methodist goes to Shabbat

During Corielle's first year at Lehigh University, I went for a Daddy-Daughter visit. Lehigh's campus is perched in the hills above Bethlehem, Pennsylvania, and as we walked through the tree lined streets, we came upon a group of boys standing outside the AEPi fraternity house. We stopped to chat, and Corielle being that cute freshman girl that gets invited to fraternity parties, we soon found ourselves invited to join them that evening, if we had no other plans, at Shabbat.

AEPi is a Jewish fraternity, but being unfamiliar with the Jewish faith, we didn't know what Shabbat was. We gathered from their remarks, though, that on this particular evening Shabbat involved eating sushi. Now, I'm a Methodist, or, perhaps more precisely, a lapsed Methodist. Except Methodists don't lapse. Catholics lapse. Methodists may stop going to church, but we don't feel guilty enough about it to refer to ourselves as lapsed. But anyway, I'm a Methodist, and maybe it isn't proper for a Methodist to go to Shabbat, but there was going to be sushi, and I like sushi.

It's been a long time since my college days, but I still remember the parties. They were always wild and smelled of spilled beer, so I admit to being taken aback when we rang the bell of a well-kept house just off campus, and instead of John Belushi a Rabbi opened the door. He sported a full black beard and wore a broad-brimmed top hat, a neck shawl, and a long black overcoat. Again, and you'll forgive me, but it's been a long time, when I was a young man, one almost never found a Rabbi hosting a fraternity party. In fact, I can't remember a single instance. But this one greeted us warmly, and if he was surprised to find a Methodist at Shabbat, he didn't let on.

Looking over his shoulder, we saw a formal dining table set up in the next room, with a group of well-dressed young men and women, all wearing yarmulkes, already seated. Clearly this was not the sushi-themed fraternity party we had been led to expect, and we tried to beg off, but the Rabbi wouldn't hear of it. "No, no! Stay!" he insisted. "Everyone is welcome. We can squeeze in two more chairs! Sit, Sit!" So we sat.

As we settled into chairs near the corner, the Rabbi's wife came around with trays of sushi for the table, and, because my momma raised me to be polite, I stood and offered my hand. "Thank you for having us into your home," I said. She looked at my hand as if there were mayonnaise on it and actually took a step backwards.

"I'm sorry," she said, "We're Orthodox. I don't shake hands."

Oh no! *Faux pas!* I hadn't been in the house five minutes and already I had insulted the Rabbi's wife!

The girl sitting to our right explained. "Orthodox women," she said, "aren't allowed to touch the skin of a man other than their husband. In fact, other men aren't even allowed to see her real hair. She's wearing a wig." For the rest of the evening, I couldn't help but imagine what her real hair might look like, and I must confess, the thought was disturbingly erotic.

Corielle and I were finishing our salads when the Rabbi called for the group's attention. This was Shabbat dinner, he explained, and as such was particularly holy. We would all be getting up now, he continued, and going to wash our hands before we began to eat. I spit a piece of salad back into the palm of my hand.

We all left the table and washed our hands, pouring water three times over the left hand and then three times over the right using a special two handled cup. I noticed there was no soap involved in this ritual, though, so it seemed to me that Methodists are perhaps even holier around mealtime, but I didn't bother to point that out.

We sat back down, and everyone tucked into salad and sushi. Corielle and I were being generous with the sushi, because you can get through a lot of that sort of thing without filling up, until the girl on our right leaned in again and whispered, "You know, there are about six courses still to come." Well, no, we hadn't known that. In fact, in hindsight, we probably shouldn't have eaten those twisty rolls that were scattered around the table, which, as it turned out, were mostly decorative anyway.

The Rabbi's wife was soon back with a platter laden with bowls of steaming Matzo Ball Soup. It is traditional, I learned then, to serve Matzo Ball Soup at precisely 211 degrees Fahrenheit. Hot enough to easily take the skin off your tongue, but not so hot as to boil in warning. I spent the next several minutes with my tongue in my glass of ice water while I blotted soup off the table and apologized to the young man across from me.

After we finished our soup, the Rabbi rose to his feet. "Everyone take up your Shabbat booklet from in front of your plate," he said, "and turn to page 147. We'll sing all verses of number twenty-seven, one of our favorites, *Shabbat Shalom*. Do you all have it? All right, with energy now!" and we all burst into song. Or they all burst into song. I hadn't found page 147 yet. As it turns out, page number one is in the very back of the book, and the numbers get bigger toward the front. By the time I found page 147, and located number twenty-seven, it came as no surprise that it was printed in Hebrew and there were no notes drawn, yet everyone was belting along as if they were singing *The Little Brown Church* at a revival meeting.

Corielle and I did our best. We joined in somewhere during the third verse. It actually wasn't so hard as long as we remembered to pronounce the "ch" as if we were clearing our throats. Every so often, the Rabbi shouted encouragement. "Come on, let me hear those wonderful voices!" and, "Let's really pick it up now!" By the end, Corielle and I were shouting out unknown lyrics and spraying spit and phlegm with the best of them. I asked the girl to our right if she understood the words to the songs we were singing. "Oh, no," she replied happily, "not at all."

And that's how it went. For the next several hours we ate chicken, and brisket, and something suspiciously like sausage, and between courses, we sang. In Hebrew. With our wonderful voices. Until, after two deserts had been brought out and consumed, we finally pushed back from the table.

As we headed for the door, I whispered to Corielle, "I'm going to hug the Rabbi's wife!" but I didn't, because, as I said before, my momma raised me to be polite, and so the evening ended without further incident.

Except I did keep the little hat they'd given me. I didn't think they'd miss it.

When in Amsterdam

We sat on the open-air upper deck of the Viking VE river cruise ship, the lights of Amsterdam floating slowly past. A man I had just met reached across from his lounge chair and offered me a joint of marijuana. I don't smoke, and certainly not marijuana, but I hesitated for just a moment and then reached out and took it.

What the hell, it had been a long day, and we were in Amsterdam after all.

Our trip had begun thirty-six hours earlier on a tiny American Eagle plane in Chicago. We were leaving from O'Hare for a three-week 'vacation of a lifetime', a Viking river cruise that sailed out of Amsterdam and finished in Budapest.

As we climbed aboard the plane, I had to stoop my head as I moved down the aisle to my seat. Three men had to be moved from the back of the plane to the front in order to balance the plane, which is apparently a real thing they have to do occasionally with small planes. There was no overhead storage space, so all carry-on luggage had to be gate-checked.

The American Eagle flew us to Baltimore, where we had a two-hour layover. The second leg of our journey took us from Baltimore to London, where we had another long layover before we made the final hop of forty-five-minutes to Amsterdam. When we finally deplaned, after a total of nearly sixteen hours of travel, we went to retrieve our luggage, which had been booked straight through from Chicago to Amsterdam. We hadn't had to handle it in either Baltimore or London, so, while Cindy waited at the luggage carousel, I went to Lost Luggage, to see if it might not have somehow arrived ahead of us.

The young woman at the service desk typed our flight information into her computer and an almost comical look of concern came over her face. I decided later that she practiced that face in front of a mirror, because apparently, she used it a lot. She told me that a report had already been filed, and our luggage had not made it onto the tiny American Eagle plane back in Chicago. It had gone instead to Dallas, and, although it was now on its way to Amsterdam, it wouldn't arrive until early tomorrow morning.

That was not a problem, I assured her. We were spending a night in Amsterdam before boarding a river cruise late tomorrow afternoon, and if they could send our luggage around to our hotel tomorrow, there would be no harm done.

"Oh, I'm so sorry," she told me. While our bags could certainly be forwarded to our hotel, she said, that process would take three or four days.

Well, that wouldn't work, I explained. Our luggage was arriving early tomorrow morning, and we weren't leaving until tomorrow evening. Our hotel was nearby, but once we embarked on the river cruise, and we had a three- or four-day head start, our luggage would never catch up with us.

I'm not sure how it was possible, but she managed to look even more sincerely concerned as she told me there was nothing more she could do.

The serious negotiating in our family is always left for Cindy. I had grown up on a farm, and on a farm, everyone does their job. There is no such thing as not getting up in the morning to milk the cows. There is no calling in sick or being hung over. No one ever says, "There's nothing more I can do," until there is honestly, literally Nothing More they can do, and even then, they won't say it. But Cindy had worked in corporate, and she knew that people often said there was nothing more that they could do, when what they really meant was, "I'm not going to try any harder than this."

So, I sighed and left to go find Cindy. I hated to do it, because this young lady seemed like a nice person, whose bodily orifices were probably of normal size, and Cindy was about to crawl right up inside one of them.

When I returned in a few moments with Cindy, it was decided, after a short but fierce negotiation, that the retrieval and delivery of our luggage would be expedited, and it would be sent to our hotel before we checked out tomorrow. We were even given a phone number that we could use to check on the status of our luggage as it made its way through the process. As we walked away from the desk, the line behind us, composed of people in situations similar to our own, had grown until it extended out the door, and our helpful young friend had fastened her concerned gaze onto the next person in line. It was an ominous sign, but one we didn't remark on until later.

We had a reservation that evening at a small boutique hotel in downtown Amsterdam, so we left the terminal and walked to the train station, which was conveniently located on a lower level of the same building. We bought a ticket at a kiosk, and it informed us that our train left from Platform C at 18:31. We walked onto Platform C at about 18:29 and jumped onto the train that soon pulled into the station.

Just to double check that we were on the correct train, we asked a lady seated across the aisle from us if this train was going to Downtown Central. She didn't speak English, unfortunately, but she understood enough to shake her head and say, "Downtown Central? No."

The man in the seat in front of us turned around and agreed, "No. Downtown Central? No."

Apparently, the 18:29 train in Amsterdam is a completely different beast from the 18:31, and if it's the 18:31 you want, you have no business getting on one at 18:29.

A girl behind us, who spoke a bit of English, chimed in and suggested that we get off at the next stop and catch the next train, which would probably take us to Downtown Central. A man from the rear of the train then came forward, and the four of them, the lady from across the aisle, the man in front, the girl behind, and the man from the rear of the train, held an animated conversation in Dutch. Finally, they agreed that yes, we should get off at the next stop and take the next train, and it would certainly take us where we wanted to go. The trip, they said, should be about ten minutes, and they hoped we hadn't been too inconvenienced by having gotten onto the wrong train.

You just don't meet people like that on the 'L' in Chicago. In Chicago, they won't get up to offer you a seat even if you're pregnant and have only one leg. But these people. We still exchange Christmas cards with all of them.

We made the transfer and found our way to Central station and from there via a five-minute walk to our hotel. Cindy woke me at ten-thirty the next morning. She had been up since six. She had taken breakfast, planned our day, and checked on our luggage, of which there was still no word.

We checked out at eleven and spent the day touring Amsterdam. It is a remarkable city, filled with canals and tulips and bicycles. And coffee shops. The coffee shops probably serve coffee, but they're famous for their offerings of marijuana and hashish. I peeked inside one, but even in college I had never partaken, and now was not a good time to start. I could barely stay out of the way of the bicyclists as it was, and if I were impaired, someone would certainly end up in a canal.

When we returned to our hotel at three that afternoon our luggage had not yet arrived, so we called the number given to us the night before at the airport. The woman who answered, by checking her computer, was able to confirm that the flight carrying our luggage had arrived in Amsterdam that morning, but beyond that, she knew nothing. When we asked if she might not take a walk around and check, she informed us that she was in London, and that there was nothing more she could do.

Time had run short, at this point. We were supposed to board the cruise ship at four, so Cindy and I made a bold plan. Cindy would take our carry-on luggage and hail a cab to the ship. I would walk back to Downtown Central, catch a train back to the airport, find my way to the British Airway's lost luggage area, retrieve our luggage, and make my way back to the cruise ship before it set sail.

Now, if you've been following along with my stories so far, you know what an audacious plan this was. I, traveling alone now, was to make my way back to a train station that I had barely found the night before while riding on a train which actually went there, and then I was to buy a ticket, which would take me, if I managed to get on the correct train, to the airport. You get the idea. Las Vegas odds-makers were not taking bets on my being on the cruise ship when it set sail later that evening.

I managed to find the train station, not because we had been there the night before, but because Cindy and I, while touring Amsterdam, had walked past it not a half hour before on our way back to the hotel. I bypassed the ticket kiosks and went to the counter to buy a ticket. The agent told me that the train to the airport left in four minutes from platform 14E. I left at a run, because, although I didn't know where platform 14E was, I knew I had *exactly* four minutes to find it.

I ran onto the platform and jumped directly into the open doors of a train. I immediately asked the first person I saw if this train went to the airport. I was assured that it did by at least six people. As the train stopped at stations along the way, I asked again and again, "Is this the stop for the airport?" When we finally arrived, the woman I had first asked for help reached out and took my elbow. "Will you be all right now?" she asked. I'm sure she thought I was part of a training program for disadvantaged adults learning to live independently.

I stopped at the information desk in the airport lobby and was told that Door number sixteen was where those seeking lost luggage must go. It seemed to be a question they answered a lot. At Door number sixteen they asked for my paperwork from the airline and my passport, which, by the purest chance, I had in my pocket, or my adventure would have ended there. After inspecting my credentials, they let me in and directed me to the British Airways lost luggage area, where our troubles had begun the night before.

Once there, I saw no familiar faces, and no one knew anything of my lost luggage. When I told them that it had arrived on a flight early that morning from Dallas, and that it was to have been expedited to our hotel, they suggested that I go look at carousel five, where the flight in question had unloaded its luggage. I was certain that the word expedite didn't involve my luggage being left for eight hours beside a baggage carousel, but I went to look.

It wasn't there.

I returned to the desk, and an agent came reluctantly around and asked that I follow him to the Storage Room to search for it there. Upon entering the room, it became clear why we hadn't begun there. This was not a room that British Airways wanted the general public to see. It was a large room, with rows and rows of shelving that extended from floor to ceiling, all filled with lost luggage. Some of it clearly from the 1960s. This was the Room of Spoiled Vacations.

I looked around for several minutes in despair, but then, with a surge of relief, I spotted my luggage in a far corner of the room. It was on the very top of a mobile cart, and I realized that in the minds of British Airways its return *was* being expedited. It hadn't been moved onto a permanent shelf. It still had hope!

"There it is!" I almost wept. "On the top of that cart."

"Ok, then," the agent said, "there you go."

"But don't you want to check my ID or something?" I asked. "Fill out some paperwork?"

The agent came over and looked at the tags on my bags. "It says Alan Heath," he said. "What's your name?"

"Alan Heath," I answered.

"There you go," he said again.

We left the room, and the agent pulled the door shut behind us. I felt saddened by those other pieces of luggage, lost and forgotten, in the dark behind that door, but at least I had my own.

I made my way out of the airport, back to the train station, and, without mishap this time, to Downtown Central. From there it was a ten-minute walk to the pier, where I found the Viking VE and came aboard with two large suitcases. The porter at the gangway greeted me. "Ah, you must be Dr. Heath. Your party is already seated at dinner. You may leave your luggage with me and join them straight away if you'd like."

I walked into a boisterous dining room and found Cindy at a noisy table for ten, which included her brother Peppy and his wife Andy along with six others, strangers only an hour before, but already fast friends. They were nearly finished with their entrees and three bottles of wine, and they greeted me happily. It was clear from their reaction to my arrival that Cindy had been preparing them for the likelihood that she would be traveling alone.

After supper, we went onto the upper deck where we relaxed in lounge chairs under the starlit sky and watched the lights of Amsterdam float slowly past. Mike, who had been one of those at our table, dug into his pocket with a mischievous grin and came out with two rolled joints. "I stopped at a coffee shop today," he said, "and I got these. Anybody care to join me?"

I hesitated for just a minute before I leaned forward and reached out my hand.

What the hell. It had been a very long day, and we were in Amsterdam after all.

I Married Nostradamus

I can admit without embarrassment that I have a bed wetting problem.

It's not a large problem, and the reason I can admit it without embarrassment is that it isn't my fault. It's Cindy's. You see, Cindy sees dead people. She comes by her gift honestly, having descended on her mother's side from a long line of similarly gifted women who appeared in skipped generations. It's even possible that some of her nameless ancestors earned a small living by their skills. Or were perhaps burned at the stake or crushed with stones.

Mostly the dead people come to Cindy at night, at the moment of their death, and they stand at the foot of my bed to say their final farewells. According to Cindy, they don't actually *say* anything though, per se, they simply project a feeling of peace and of departing to a better place. The following day, when Cindy hears that the Dearly Beloved has become the Dearly Departed, she will ask, "Was it about, say, 2:37ish that they passed away?" and the bereaved will take several steps back and their hair will stand on end.

But the reaction of the bereaved is nothing compared to the effect that these nocturnal farewells have on me, the innocent bystander. Many is the time I've been awakened in the middle of the night by Cindy sitting bolt upright and staring at the foot of our bed like a dog growling at an empty closet. I sit up and look franticly around the empty bedroom. "Cindy," I whisper, "there's no one here," but she raises a trembling finger and points dramatically toward the foot of the bed before collapsing back onto her pillow in a deep, trance-like sleep, and I'm left lying in suddenly dampened sheets.

Cindy considers these final moments to be a special blessing which she can share with loved ones left behind, but I personally find them useless, at least as prophetic visitations go. It isn't as if any of them have ever taken the time to to tell Cindy, "Oh, and by the way, buy *Google*," which would at least be useful information, and, honestly, they've come all this way, how much longer would it take?

But occasionally Cindy puts her powers to better use. Years ago, as an example, we were living in a townhouse in Frankfort Square, and it had a small basement. The sump pump ran continuously whenever it rained. When we eventually finished the basement and laid some nice carpet, I decided that a battery backup for our sump pump would be a good investment. I installed the pump, but no battery was purchased to go with it, and for several weeks the new pump sat with its battery cables dangling uselessly. Finally, one Saturday morning, Cindy got up and said, "We have to get a battery for that sump pump today. I had a dream last night that it was pouring rain, and the basement was flooded, and we were carrying buckets of water to the second floor and emptying them into the bathtub."

Well, that was ridiculous, because who in their right mind would walk right past the sink in the kitchen and carry buckets of water to the second floor to empty them into a bathtub? But I had learned not to ignore Cindy's dreams, so we soon found ourselves at J.C. Penny's buying a marine battery.

"Now, this battery," the salesman said, "as she sits right now, isn't charged up, but I can put her on the charger for you, and she'll be ready by the time we close tonight, or you can come back tomorrow and pick her up."

"That's fine," I said. "We'll pick it up in the morning," and I turned to look at Cindy, who was giving me her Nostradamus look, which involves mostly just her left eye, and I turned back to the salesman.

"How late did you say you were open tonight?" I asked.

We came back at nine PM and picked up the battery. I hooked it up at ten, it started to rain at midnight, and the power went out at one. The battery backup ran all night long. We didn't have to carry a single bucket of water up to the second floor and empty it into the bathtub, which, no matter how ridiculous it might sound, is almost certainly what we would have done.

Now, I've told you all of that so that I can tell you this.

We were on our way to a birthday party at our friend Eileen's house, and as we drove down White Street, Cindy turned to me and said casually, "I had the strangest dream last night."

The hair stood up on the back of my neck.

"I dreamed I had a dog." Cindy said wistfully.

To be honest, I would have preferred that someone had died. I'm not a man who tolerates change easily you see, and although I grew up on a farm surrounded by dogs and cats and the occasional raccoon, for nearly forty years we'd been a house with no pets. We'd never been *able* to have a pet because Cindy is violently allergic to dogs, cats, and, I assume, raccoons. "You," I reminded her, "are allergic to dogs."

"Not this one," she said. "It's name was Coco, and it was adorable. Tiny and fluffy white. I was holding it up under my chin, and it was licking my face. I wasn't allergic to it at all. And in my dream you were being mean to me and telling me "You can't have a dog! You're allergic to dogs." Cindy sighed. "I would love to have a dog," she said.

We had been at the party only a few minutes when Eileen walked into the room holding a small, fluffy, white dog. "Al," Cindy whispered, poking me to get my attention, "that's exactly like the dog in my dream!" Eileen casually lifted the dog up under her chin and cuddled it. The dog licked her chin. "That's exactly how I was holding the dog in my dream," Cindy said excitedly.

"All right," I sighed, "hold the dog."

We had been through this scenario before, with friends who had designer dogs with names like Cockapoo, that allergic people weren't supposed to be allergic to, but Cindy always was, so I still nurtured the hope that the night might end with a life-threatening anaphylactic episode and a trip to the emergency room.

Cindy took the dog from Eileen and held it in her lap. Minutes passed. She lifted the dog up under her chin and ruffled her face into its fur. The dog twisted in her arms and licked her chin. Nothing happened. No itching. No welt. No wheezing or sneezing. No anaphylaxis. Cindy looked at me with delight. "I'm not allergic to this dog!" She exclaimed.

"You can't have a dog," I blurted, with a desperate crack in my voice, "You're allergic to dogs!"

"That's just what you said in my dream," Cindy whispered, and she looked at me with just her left eye.

And I wet myself a little bit.

Cindy holding Coco. Just like in her dream!

There's a Snake in Our Backyard

We were taking Tony to Nashville for the start of term at Vanderbilt. The drive was too far to go down and back in a single day, so our friends, Pat and Steve, who lived in Franklin, a prosperous and historic suburb just outside of Nashville, had offered to let us spend the night with them. After we dropped Tony off at school we drove out to Franklin, and they fed us a meal and tucked us into a guest bedroom for the night.

I was the first one up the next day, and I went for an early morning walk. Along the way I spotted a Garage Sale sign. Browsing through boxes of old video games, children's toys, and baby clothes, I stumbled across an articulated wooden snake. It was very lifelike, eighteen inches long, with an alternate red, black, and yellow segmented body. It lay coiled in the bottom of the box. It hissed my name.

For 50 cents I walked away with a snake in my pocket and an evil plan in my head.

When I returned from my walk, I found Pat and her sister Cheryl sitting in the garage, sharing a cigarette and a cup of coffee. The overhead garage doors were open, as was the back door leading onto the patio. I passed through the garage with a brief "good morning" and went onto the patio. At the edge of the lawn stood several large planters, and I coiled my snake at the base of the nearest, so that it appeared to be slithering out of the grass and onto the brick. And that was the extent of my evil plan. I was content to know that at some point in the next several days, someone would discover the snake, and hilarity would ensue. The fact that I wouldn't be there to enjoy it bothered me not in the least.

With the snake in position, I went back into the garage, pulled up a lawn chair, and poured myself a mug of coffee. We had sat for only a few minutes when Pat's husband Steve appeared. He was dragging a garden hose through the garage from the driveway, apparently intent on watering the flowers on the patio. I sat up straighter in my chair and waited with bated breath as Steve disappeared onto the patio with his hose.

Moments later, Steve reappeared in the open doorway, gliding backwards in a fair approximation of Michael Jackson's moonwalk. He held the trickling garden hose in a limp right hand. As he passed the door, his head, with eyes big as saucers, snapped left. "There's a snake in our backyard!" he announced with amazing calm, and he disappeared out of sight beyond the doorway.

Cheryl and Pat reacted as if someone had set fire to the garage. They leapt to their feet, upsetting their chairs and spilling their coffee. "There's a snake in our backyard?" Pat shouted in a voice tinged with hysteria. "There's never been a snake in our backyard before!" and they both ran to the door and poked their heads through, one above the other, all the while keeping the bulk of themselves safely within the protective confines of the garage.

"Where?" Pat cried, "I don't see it. Where is it?"

Cheryl pointed, "Oh my God, there it is. Over by the flowerpot!" Her voice rose in pitch throughout this speech, so that only dogs heard the part about the flowerpot. I couldn't believe my good fortune. Not only was I here to witness my evil plan bear fruit, but apparently both girls were pathologically afraid of snakes.

"How big is it?" I asked, by way of throwing gasoline on the fire.

"It's really big," Pat said, and she turned to look as I began rummaging through a heap of tools lying in a corner of the garage. "Oh no!" she quavered, "What are you going to do with that?"

I didn't answer as I pushed past the girls and went out onto the patio, bravely gripping a hoe with both hands. Pat began to whimper. "Oh, please no, Al. Don't do that. Oh please..." I advanced, crab-like, toward the flowerpot indicated by Steve's trembling finger. Pat was openly sobbing now. Six feet from the snake, I stopped and straightened up. "Why, that's not even a poisonous snake," I said, and I lay down the hoe and took two more cautious steps toward it. I could hear Pat choke as I lowered myself into a crouch.

"No, please no, please no, please no!" Pat had taken a death grip on Cheryl's arm, and was incoherent with fear. I reached slowly forward and held my hand poised above the wooden viper. With a sudden lunge, too quick for the eye to follow, I struck, snatching the snake from the ground and in one motion holding it aloft at arm's length. The articulated snake writhed in a lifelike fashion. Pat screamed, turned, and fled into the house, slamming the door behind her. Unfortunately, she kept her grip on Cheryl's arm throughout, causing consternation and confusion as she stood inside, still screaming, and hysterically trying to force the door shut on her sister's arm.

Gradually, reason returned to all involved, and I explained how a wooden snake had come to be on their patio that morning. I also apologized. If I had known, I said, that Pat had such an unreasoned fear of snakes, I would never have done what I did—without setting up video equipment first.

Show Me Your Finger

It was just after New Year's, and Cindy and I, along with the kids, who were home from college, were vacationing at the Lawrence Welk Resort just north of San Diego.

The Lawrence Welk is a quiet, family-style resort, and they have a little bar that seats about twelve next to the Canyon Grill restaurant. The bar is never crowded, and on the night of the Orange Bowl, we decided to go down for drinks and a burger while we watched the game on their big screen TV.

I went down first. Cindy, Corielle, and Tony were going to follow directly. When I entered the bar, I was surprised to find several small groups filling the chairs and only two open seats. I slid into one, but before I could lay claim to the second a middle-aged woman sat down beside me. I glanced at the other groups, checking to see who looked as if they might be about ready to leave. A couple seated several chairs further down the bar returned my look and raised their glasses. "Welcome," the woman said. "My name's Laura, and this is my friend Riley. Where are you from?"

"My name's Al. From Chicago," I said with a friendly tilt of my glass. The game was about to begin, and I looked back at the TV.

"Are you staying at the resort, Al?" Laura asked. "Riley and I live nearby, just up the mountain a bit."

"Yes," I answered, with one eye still on the TV, "I'm here for the week."

At about that time, the woman who had sat down with me got up and moved off toward the restaurant. "Oh, I'm sorry," said Laura with a look of concern. "I shouldn't have spoken across her like that. That was rude of me. Have I offended her?"

"Who?" I asked, laying claim to the empty chair by throwing my left arm possessively across its back.

"Your date," Laura answered, with a nod in the direction of the retreating woman.

"Oh," I said, "I don't know her. We just came in at the same time. We came in alone together." I realized I wasn't making much sense, so I gave her an apologetic smile as I turned back to the game. "I'm here alone," I clarified.

"Oh," she said, and she was silent for a moment. "Why do you wear your ring on that finger?" she asked. I looked back and saw that she was pointing to the middle finger of my left hand, which still lay across the empty chair back.

Now, I should explain, I suppose, that I don't wear my wedding band on the ring finger of my left hand. That finger has a knuckle swollen to gargantuan proportions, so I wear my ring on the middle finger instead. When I made the switch twenty years ago, I assumed no one would notice. I certainly wouldn't have. But then, I'm not the most observant of men. Cindy could come home from the hairdresser with her head shaved, and although I would notice the change, I wouldn't remark on it for fear she had done it several days ago, and it had only just now caught my eye.

But apparently some people are more attuned than I to the minutia of ring finger etiquette. Laura continued to look at me expectantly, but my knuckle's story is a long one, and rather than go into it, I gave her a noncommittal shrug and turned back to the game. I assumed that

that would be the end to it, but Laura was undeterred. Over the next five minutes, she continued to chatter away while I did my best to listen politely while keeping one ear and an eye on the football game.

Laura was Irish, I learned, which she suspected I was as well, by the color of my eyes and the hint of an accent which she claimed to hear when I said certain words. She and Riley shared a house in the hills, where they were roommates, but nothing more. "We're best friends," Laura announced.

"That's right," Riley confirmed, "we've been roommates for ten years, but we're just friends. It works out great."

Laura grew roses in a garden behind her house. Hundreds of roses that she grafted onto wild stem stock, and I was welcome to come see them if I'd like. By now I had resigned myself to the fact that I wasn't going to see much of the game, and Laura, Riley, and I were discussing the merits of keeping raccoons as pets when Corielle and Tony finally came in.

I did the introductions.

Laura had been calling me Dental Boy ever since she had extracted what I did for a living, and I had taken to calling her Irish Rose. "Kids," I said, "this is Laura, the Irish Rose, and this is her friend Riley."

"That's right," Riley announced. "We're friends. Roommates for ten years, but nothing more than that between us." Corielle looked with concern from Laura and Riley to me while Laura scurried around the room pulling chairs up to the bar to make room for the kids.

"Who is she?" Corielle whispered.

"I don't know," I said. "She lives near here, and she grows roses. Which we are invited to go see, if you'd like." Corielle arched an eyebrow and gave me an odd look as I turned back to the game and tried to bring Tony up to speed on the progress of the first quarter. My attention was pulled away by a light slap against the back of my head.

"You didn't say you had such beautiful children, Dental Boy," Laura scolded. She had finished collecting chairs and was standing between Tony and me.

"I meant to," I said. "In fact, I was just about to say what beautiful children I had when they came in."

"Liar," Laura said, and she punched me playfully in the chest. She left her hand lying against my chest as she circled around me to Corielle. "You're a beautiful girl," she said, and then she leaned closer and lowered her voice to a confidential whisper. "What happened to your mother?"

"My mother?" Corielle asked.

"Yes, I'm so sorry. What happened to her?" Laura persisted.

"I don't know," Corielle said. "Did something happen to her?"

"You poor thing," consoled Laura. "Has she been gone long?"

"No, not long," Corielle answered. "She's just back in the room. She'll be down in a few minutes." Laura staggered back and jerked her arm from around my chest as if she had been burned. She threw a horrified look in my direction before dashing back to her seat. After a moment she leaned across to Corielle, "I'm so sorry," she whispered.

Just then Cindy walked into the bar and came to lean against the back of my chair. I gave her a quick kiss. Laura got up and walked unsteadily toward Cindy, who took an uneasy step backwards before Laura folded her into a hug. "You have a beautiful family!" Laura sobbed. I looked back from the game to find Laura and Cindy wrapped in each other's arms. Laura was glaring at me over Cindy's shoulder, and she was showing me the middle finger of each hand.

Neither finger had a ring on it.

A Small, White, Fluffy Dog

I'm man who's comfortable with his sexuality. A man who can lead a small, white, fluffy dog on a pink retractable leash and not feel compelled to apologize. A man who lets his testosterone speak for itself.

Recently, it came to Cindy in a dream that we would own a dog, and its name would be Coco, and her prophecy has been fulfilled. Coco is a Bichon Frise, and she's not the sort of a dog that wears a metal-studded collar chained to a tire in the back yard. She's a tiny ball of white fluff, with boot button eyes and a laughing mouth that small children rush up to and say, "Oh! What a cute puppy."

Coco is Cindy's first dog, but I grew up surrounded by dogs. Dogs named Shepp or Bear, that slept in the barn next to the cows. Farm dogs. Large dogs, with rough, ungroomed coats that as often as not smell of skunk. With huge heads, the size of hams, and gaping, slobbering jaws. Salesmen backed around and left rather than get out of their cars when confronted by a farm dog.

And now I have a dog once again, but if you put a broom handle up her butt, she would look like a Q-tip. A very indignant Q-tip, but you get the picture, I hope.

Coco has registration papers listing both mother and father going back several generations. She weighs twelve pounds, and I wash her hair as often as I wash my own. She's a healthy puppy, and yet she's run up veterinary bills of hundreds of dollars. I don't know the exact dollar value of this veterinary care, because Cindy feels that on my current level of medication its best that I'm not told. Coco doesn't run outside, and yet we dose her with flea and tick repellant. She's never off a leash, and yet we've had a microchip implanted beneath her skin for identification. We've paid to have her toenails clipped, and I've been informed that she'll need haircuts on a regular basis. But again, the magnitude of this expense is on a need-to-know basis, and I don't need to know.

We took her to a dog obedience class, but we're thinking now of Home Schooling. Not that there's anything wrong with the public school system, it's just that we want what's best for Coco. We shop regularly at a little boutique for dogs in downtown Frankfort, where we spend untold numbers of discretionary dollars on leashes, toys, treats, and gourmet dog foods. Her Halloween costume was adorable, and she has a winter jacket with little booties for when the weather turns colder.

Patty, our next-door neighbor, waved me over from her driveway. "Al," she called, "you got a puppy?" I was taking Coco for one of her first walks, and she was floating at the end of her leash, like a ball of lint caught in an updraft.

"This is Coco," I said.

"She's wearing a pink outfit," Patty said, pointing to Coco's sweater.

"It's chilly," I explained. And then, in an effort to redirect the conversation, I said, "we use a retractable leash with a body harness instead of a collar."

"Also pink," Patty pointed out, not to be sidetracked. "And that?" she asked, pointing to a flask on my hip.

"It's a water bottle," I answered, now a little uneasy with the direction of her questioning.

"Again, Al, it's pink," she continued. "How far are you going that you'll need water?"

"It's for Coco," I explained.

Patty rolled her eyes. "And what, exactly, is that?" she asked finally, pointing to a small container clipped to my belt.

"It holds poopy pouches," I admitted sheepishly.

Patti giggled. "Al, it's a tiny pink purse."

"It holds poopy pouches," I repeated stubbornly. "You have to clean up after your dog!"

"Al," Patty laughed, "you've accessorized your puppy!"

I scooped Coco up under one arm.

"Come on Coco," I huffed. "We don't have to stand here and listen to this. Daddy thinks you're a pretty girl. Yes you are!" And I stormed away.

I'd have stayed longer, but I'm the kind of man who lets his testosterone speak for itself, and my testosterone couldn't think of anything else to say.

Stop This at Once!

I'm not a child, but I own toys. And I'm not talking about big-boy toys, like fancy golf clubs or a pick-up truck. I'm talking about toys.

For example, I own both a potato cannon and a water balloon slingshot. Both are useless for purposes of hunting or home protection. You can imagine the futility of waking up in the middle of the night, elbowing your spouse and whispering, "Honey, I hear a noise! Go get a potato or fill a water balloon!" but that isn't why I have them. They're toys.

The water balloon slingshot takes three people to operate. Two of them hold the handles of a large rubber band, six feet across with a canvas pouch in the center. The third loads a balloon into the pouch, stretches the band, and launches the balloon. Done properly, a watery payload can be delivered to a distance of one hundred yards with reasonable accuracy. On a golf course, the reaction of a golfer as he lines up a putt and is interrupted by a water balloon falling out of the clear blue sky is worth the price of the greens fee.

Some friends and I once spent an entire morning trying to drop a water balloon into George Van Dyke's lap as he crisscrossed his lawn on his riding mower. George lived at the end of the block, which was easily within range, but he was a moving target, and as we grew frustrated, we moved closer. Finally, we were standing directly across the street and launching lasers beams from point blank range. If we had succeeded in putting a water balloon into George's ear, which had become our goal, we would have knocked him completely off his rider.

We gave up trying to hit George only when we spotted the Murphy girls playing on the driveway in front of their house. The Murphy girls lived on the cul-de-sac just across from our house, and I'm not sure exactly how many of them there were. They were never still long enough to count, but it was in the neighborhood of six or seven, and they all seemed to be under the age of five. Suffice it to say, their driveway was saturated with little girls. In the military, that's referred to as a target-rich-environment, so we turned our attention from George and began to lob balloons onto the Murphys' driveway. The results were immediate and entertaining, as small girls squealed and dashed about in all directions.

Unfortunately, the girls were being watched that day by their Grandpa, a gentleman originally from Armenia, who took a very dim view of water balloon attacks. He hurried to the end of the driveway and peered quickly up and down the street. Spotting us, he shouted, "You people there! Stop this at once! Stop it at once, or I shall telephone the Police!"

So, appropriately chastened, we put away the water balloons. And got out the potato cannon.

Now, a potato cannon is just what it sounds like - a cannon that fires potatoes. It works with most root vegetables, but potatoes are the popular choice. The cannon is made of two-inch PVC piping, and it uses an aerosol spray in a combustion chamber for the propellant.

Unlike a water balloon slingshot, where the object is to hit someone with the water balloon, it's best that you don't hit anyone with a potato. My brother and I once shot an Idaho Red, in a carefully controlled scientific experiment, completely through the side of an outhouse.

If we had tried to knock George off his mower using the potato cannon, we would have gotten the job done. But that would have been irresponsible and possibly even wrong, and I would have felt obliged to mow George's lawn while he was in the hospital, and Mrs. Van Dyke would never have been able to serve potato salad again without George diving under a table.

So instead, we played a game of Potato Cannon 500, in which two of us stood in my driveway and launched potatoes over the neighbor's house into a field some two hundred yards distant, while the rest of our group stood in the field wearing baseball gloves and helmets and tried to catch the potatoes as they fell from the sky.

Ron and Patti Rossetto, the neighbors over whose house we were shooting, weren't home, so we didn't have to apologize or ask permission, and after Grandpa Murphy hurried the girls inside, we had the cul-de-sac to ourselves as we shot off an entire ten-pound sack of potatoes.

We finally came to the last potato, a small, wrinkled specimen that had been tossed aside earlier. It was too small to be an effective projectile, but it was the last one, and my mother had taught me not to waste food, and this fell loosely into that category. We dropped it down the barrel of the cannon and filled the ignition chamber with Right Guard, but when we pulled the trigger, instead of a satisfying "whump", we heard the subdued belch of a misfire. The potato fluttered out of the cannon and barely cleared the Rossettos' roof.

Judging by its trajectory, we knew it had landed on their patio, and the thought of that bit of forensic evidence being discovered later by the Rossettos filled us with guilt. Perhaps we had felt, on a subconscious level, ever since Grandpa Murphy had threatened us with the police, that what we were doing was somehow wrong. We hurried next door, like kids trying to hide the pieces of a broken lamp. We searched in flowerpots and under lawn furniture, but the potato had completely disappeared, and we finally gave it up for lost.

The next morning though, as I gathered the newspaper from the end of the driveway, I heard Patti calling to Ron from their backyard. "I'm telling you it's a potato!" she shouted. "How did a potato get into our hot tub?"

I slunk back into the house without saying a word, like the guilty child that I apparently was, and the only reason I'm telling you this now is that the statute of limitations has passed. If Ron and Patti were to come over now, and confront me with a wrinkled potato, I could cast my eyes down, scuff my toe against the ground, and mumble, "We was just playin'," and that would be the end of it. The police wouldn't have to be involved.

If we had hit George with a potato, I would have had to wait another ten years before telling this story.

Epilogue

It was nearly forty years ago that I first sat in my soon-to-be dental office and waited for the delivery of my dental chair and x-ray machine. Now the date for my retirement was drawing near, and I was driving home from the office at the end of the day. It was snowing. Large flakes blurred the landmarks, and my mind was back in the office with patients I'd been seeing forever and had now probably seen for the last time. Although the drive home was less than two miles, with my mind wandering and the snow swirling, I missed my turn. Suddenly a stoplight loomed out of the snow, and I realized I had gone a mile out of my way. As I made a U turn, I remembered a similar experience the very first time I drove to Frankfort.

It was one of those foggy nights that make you feel as if you're driving through a bowl of cotton candy. The world loomed into view out of the mist and disappeared as suddenly. Cindy and I had been in the car for what seemed like hours, our sense of time as well as our sense of location upset by the fog.

It was the spring of 1981, and I was finishing my Residency year at Michael Reese hospital. We were on our way to visit a prospective location to begin my dental practice. Cheryl Kosek, a hygienist in the hospital Dental Clinic, had told me about an opportunity in the little town of Frankfort. Cheryl's husband was doing an internship with a Frankfort Optometrist who had just built a professional building, and the building was looking for tenants.

"Frankfort is a lovely town," Cheryl enthused. "It's an old German farming community with a quaint, historic downtown. It would be a great place to start a dental practice. And it's growing. There's a new McDonald's going in," she said. "McDonald's does a lot of demographic studies to decide where to open new locations, and if Frankfort's growing fast enough to suit them, it should be perfect for you."

I liked the idea of a of a small rural town. I'd left the farm nine years earlier, and although I no longer had cow manure stuck to my shoes, I knew I would never be comfortable in the city.

Cindy and I made some calls. First, to the Frankfort Chamber of Commerce to get a feel for the local business environment. The phone rang for almost a minute before someone picked it up. "Hello?" a voice answered.

"Is this the Frankfort Chamber of Commerce?" I asked. "I'd like some information about your town."

"Oh, I'm sorry," the voice apologized. "She's out to lunch right now."

"Who is?" I asked, confused. "The Chamber of Commerce is out to lunch right now?"

"Yes, she is. You could call back in about forty-five minutes. She should be back by then."

I had always had the idea that a Chamber of Commerce was an organization, and if I had to assign a pronoun, I would have chosen "it" or perhaps "they." And I would not expect to find it out to lunch. But apparently the Frankfort Chamber of Commerce, rather than being large and impersonal, had gender and personality. And she took lunch at a reasonable hour. After I hung up the phone I turned to Cindy. "I think I'm going to like Frankfort," I said. "I feel like I just called home."

Next, we talked to Dr. Finnegan, the Optometrist who was building the new office, and we made plans to meet the following evening. Now, we'd been driving through the fog for what seemed like forever, on our way to visit Frankfort for the first time.

Cindy had some idea of Frankfort's general location, having grown up in Chicago Heights, eleven miles to the east. She and her friends had occasionally gone on dates to a Mexican restaurant near Frankfort, and she remembered it as having been "a long way out in the country." We had exited the expressway onto Lincoln Highway some time ago, and we'd passed a sign that read, "Frankfort – Three Miles." Now, as we drove slowly and peered through the fog, that seemed to have been ten miles ago. Suddenly another sign loomed into view for an instant before disappearing behind us. "Frankfort Public Library," it said.

I looked around in confusion. There was no sign of any sort of building or town center. No stop signs. No streetlights. Nothing. "We must be there," I exclaimed. "If that was the library, we must be there! Libraries aren't out in the middle of nowhere. They're in the center of town. But where's the town?"

We crept along for another two miles before we finally came to a stop light and a sign welcoming us to Frankfort. We found Dr. Finnegan waiting in a parking lot, and after a tour of his building and a cup of coffee with a piece of pie at the Village Restaurant, we made our decision. Frankfort was going to be our new home.

Six months later we were invited to dinner at the home of Dr. Biel, the old established dentist in town. As we sat over desert, I told the story of our drive through the fog on our first visit to Frankfort. "After we passed the sign that said 'Library'," I laughed, "we thought we had to be in the middle of town! I mean, who puts a library two miles out in the middle of nowhere?"

Dr. Biel's wife Sandy sat up straighter with an offended expression. "That was me," she huffed. "We needed a place for the new library, and no space was available downtown. And you just watch! The way this town is growing, that Library's going to be right in the middle of town soon."

That was forty years ago. And Frankfort turned out to be everything we'd hoped. It was a farm town that was growing up, and we grew with it. The people in town, strangers to begin with, became neighbors, patients, and friends. The lady at the Chamber of Commerce, once she came back from lunch, was a patient for thirty years.

Most dental patients come to the office twice a year, so at retirement the goodbyes are long and strung out. There isn't a cake, a balloon, and a ride into the sunset. It's a six-month-long handshake. Some of the patients come in with tears in their eyes, and some of those are the ones who told me years ago that they hated the dentist.

The years flew past, mostly unnoticed, but every once in awhile I became aware of them. A four-year-old girl stood facing backwards on the seat of my dental chair with her chin on the headrest as she watched me walking behind her. It was an adorable image that locked itself away in my mind. A short time later the same little girl, older now, ran into my office. "Dr. Heath!" she exclaimed. "Look in the parking lot! That's the car I'm taking to college when I leave tomorrow."

"Nice," I said, but my mind was reeling. "You're four years old!" I thought. "When did this happen? Where did the years go?"

Sonnet Corkery stood at the front desk after her appointment. "Dr. Heath," she said, "I can't believe you're retiring. No one but you has ever worked on my teeth." She was wearing a tailored business suit and looked every inch the young professional that she was.

"I know," I said with a smile. "Do you remember the first time you came into my office? You were four years old, and you wouldn't say a word the whole time you were in the chair. And then, just before you left, you peeked out from behind your Mom's skirt, and you called me a Big Jerk."

"Yeah," she laughed, "I remember."

There have been so many like Sonnet, who have grown up in my office. Almost like family. And the McDonald's corporation was right. Frankfort has grown as well, but Mrs. Biel would be disappointed. The Library is still way out in the middle of nowhere.

And I thank God for that. I like this town just the way it is.

When you retire, you miss your work. But not all the time.

CPSIA information can be obtained
at www.ICGtesting.com
Printed in the USA
LVHW012336290321
682892LV00011B/431